PENGUIN BOOKS

THE PRIMAL CHEESEBURGER

Elisabeth Rozin was born in New York City. She received a bachelor's degree from Hunter College and a master's from Brandeis University. A love of travel, cooking, and eating led to her interest in food history and a fascination with the universal aspects of culinary practices. Her first book was *The Flavor-Principle Cookbook*, published in 1973, followed by *Ethnic Cuisine* in 1983 and *Blue Corn and Chocolate* in 1992. Ms. Rozin lectures widely and is a frequent consultant to the food industry. She has four children and lives in Havertown, Pennsylvania, where she is currently working on a new cookbook, titled *The Universal Kitchen*.

THE
PRIMAL
CHEESEBURGER

Elisabeth Rozin

PENGUIN BOOKS

PENGUIN BOOKS
Published by the Penguin Group
Penguin Books USA Inc., 375 Hudson Street,
New York, New York 10014, U.S.A.
Penguin Books Ltd, 27 Wrights Lane,
London W8 5TZ, England
Penguin Books Australia Ltd, Ringwood,
Victoria, Australia
Penguin Books Canada Ltd, 10 Alcorn Avenue,
Toronto, Ontario, Canada M4V 3B2
Penguin Books (N.Z.) Ltd, 182-190 Wairau Road,
Auckland 10, New Zealand

Penguin Books Ltd, Registered Offices:
Harmondsworth, Middlesex, England
First published in Penguin Books 1994

1 3 5 7 9 10 8 6 4 2

Portions of this book first appeared in the following publications by the author: *Blue Corn and Chocolate* (Knopf), *Ethnic Cuisine* (Penguin), *The Flavor-Principle Cookbook* (Hawthorn), "The Great Ketchup-Salsa Debate" published in *Icarus*, and "Ketchup and the Collective Unconscious" in *The Journal of Gastronomy*.

Grateful acknowledgment is made for permission to reprint T. A. Layton's recipe for cheeseburgers from *The Cheese Handbook: A Guide to the World's Best Cheeses*, by T. A. Layton. By permission of Dover Publications, Inc.

LIBRARY OF CONGRESS CATALOGING IN PUBLICATION DATA
Rozin, Elisabeth.
The primal cheeseburger/ Elisabeth Rozin.
p.   cm.
Includes bibliographical references and index.
ISBN 0 14 01.7843 0
1. Hamburgers—History. 2. Condiments—History. I. Title.
GT2868.5.R69 1994
394.1'2—dc20   94-14554
Printed in the United States of America
Set in Cloister
Designed by Brian Mulligan

ACKNOWLEDGMENTS

I am grateful as always for the support, encouragement, and enthusiasm of my family and friends. Special thanks are due to Marcy B. Stricker, who gave many wise and thoughtful comments, and to Dr. Marcia Pelchat of the Monell Chemical Senses Center, who provided much helpful advice and information. This book is a better one because of these two smart and generous friends.

CONTENTS

THE
PRIMAL
CHEESEBURGER

Be cautious how you change old bills of fare,
Such alterations should at least be rare;
Yet credit to the artist will accrue,
Who in known things still makes th'appearance new.

William King (1663–1712)
*The Art of Cookery; in imitation
of Horace's Art of Poetry*

INTRODUCTION: THE UNIVERSAL MEAL

Recently a national news magazine reported the delightful story of a six-year-old Japanese boy brought by his parents for a visit to the United States. Riding from the airport, the child exclaimed with great excitement: "Look! Look! They have McDonald's here too!"

That innocent ethnocentrism evokes an indulgent chuckle, for who but a naive child does not know that McDonald's and all it purveys is fundamentally American, the very essence of who we are? Who among us does not recognize McDonald's as a powerful gustatory symbol, the ubiquitous emblem of this proud and possessive nation of burger eaters?

But the love of hamburgers, fries, and ketchup is not uniquely American, as the little Japanese boy's response so clearly indicates. The fact is that McDonald's and its greasy fraternity of Big Boys, Burger Kings, and Wendy's have established themselves throughout the world, popularizing an American classic with greater success than that of any other, including Micky Mouse, baseball, and the "Star-Spangled

Banner." The golden arches and their ilk rise not only in the bustling streets of Japan but also along the cypress-lined hills of the Aegean and the thronged waterways of Thailand, in the clamorous circus of Piccadilly, the boulevards of Mexico City, and most recently in those hitherto staunch bastions of anti-Americanism, Moscow and Beijing. Even, yes, in the Champs-Elysées, shoulder to shoulder with fashionable bistros and three-star establishments, the burger franchises ply their wares with as great an ease, it would seem, to the elitist French, long-acknowledged arbiters of gastronomy, as to voracious teenagers in the malls and minimarts of America.

This book is not about McDonald's or its brotherhood of fast-food enterprises; nor is it about marketing, merchandising, or fast food per se. It is about the food itself—so wholly American in its origin and presentation—which has been overwhelmingly accepted and adopted by a stunning diversity of cultures throughout the world. More than pricing, packaging, or prestige seems to be at work here, for the food succeeds in areas where other aspects of American culture are not very highly esteemed and in countries where it is neither fast nor cheap. The amazing popularity of the burger platter cuts across ethnic and cultural lines, appealing to a very wide variety of food tastes and traditions. What is it about this particular assemblage of foods that seems to provide such a positive experience for so many people?

Let's look at the arrangement, the platter, the meal that has so captivated the world's palate. It consists of a grilled or broiled ground beef patty, served on a soft white refined-wheat-flour bun, topped with a slice of processed "American" cheese, spread with ketchup, and garnished with onions, pickles, lettuce, and tomato. This warm layered sandwich is served with a portion of french fried potatoes and washed down with a cold sweet carbonated drink, most commonly a Coke. And that's it. Nothing complicated, nothing subtle, nothing extravagant, nothing provocative. But the beauty of this simple meal, its certain appeal, is that it provides something for everyone. Its various parts recapitulate much that is central and common to the human food experience.

Humans are culinary animals: We cook our food, we mess around with it, we season it, we change it, and we have done so from the very earliest times. Indeed, cooking, like language or art, is one of those fundamental behaviors that define us as human and distinguish us from other animals. In Western mythology, the metaphor for that crucial shift from innocent creaturehood to true humanness is the expulsion of Adam and Eve from the Garden of Eden. Disobedience to God, knowledge, and the assumption of free will forced humans to leave Paradise, with its wealth of fruits and nuts; deprived them of the luxury of picking dinner off a tree; and drove them into a world where food had to be gathered, hunted, wrested from the soil—and cooked: "In the sweat of your brow you shall eat bread."

And so, as full (and fallen) humans, we hunted and gathered, and later we planted and harvested and pastured. But always we cooked. And the interesting thing is that no matter how widely divergent we became, in terms of geography and culture, we all seemed to eat the same kinds of things and to cook or prepare them in very similar ways. From time to time and place to place the details of the enterprise varied, as they still do, but the basic foods and the techniques remained the same—a testament to both the consistency and the specialness of our species.

Almost everything that has been learned or practiced in the long human history of food can be accounted for in the seemingly simple components of the burger platter. No matter who we are or where we come from, we can find something in that meal that evokes a sense of belonging, of participation, in a universal human enterprise—a flavor, a texture, an aroma, a mouth experience that seems to provide pleasure, familiarity, and a feeling of well-being. The cheeseburger is a thoroughly contemporary American phenomenon, but it is primal in its capacity to evoke a collective—and positive—human experience. Surely it is no accident that such a dramatic and sensory recapitulation of our past should have developed in a place where the accumulated people and traditions of all history came together for the first time on one soil. If the melting pot exists, the cheeseburger may well be its most palpable product; to take a bite of it is to take a bite of history and to experience in a mouthful what we have wished for, and upon, ourselves.

One

THE
GROUND BEEF
PATTY

I t is, for nearly everyone, love at first bite. Interviewed for American television at the recent opening of Moscow's first McDonald's, a Russian woman wiped her lips and crooned: "Oh, the meat! It's so soft, so delicious!" That reaction was not very different from one that I elicited when I recently visited Indonesia. I asked a young woman who lives in the capital city of Djakarta whether she had sampled the food of the many fast-food emporia that sprout like mushrooms through the smog of the urban Asian sprawl. Her eyes lit up with remembered pleasure as she assured me that, yes, she indulged quite often in the delights of the cheeseburger platter and that she loved everything about it, but most especially the burger itself. "The meat is so *good!*" she said, and her enthusiastic appreciation was clear.

Given the vast differences, both cultural and geographic, between Russia and Indonesia, those responses were amazingly similar, and both, interestingly, focused on the meat. That is a little curious because, unlike the burgers we Americans consume at backyard barbecues or enjoy in somewhat more upscale restaurants, the meat portion of the burger platter as presented by the fast-food franchises is not very significant in terms of its volume or its visual impact. It is but one slender layer, barely visible, and yet it holds the stage as the central and most critical ingredient. The ground beef patty, no matter how skimpy, no matter what variety of foods surround and accompany it, remains the focus and the organizing principle in the construction and the significance of the cheeseburger platter. And therein lies the tale.

Whatever our contemporary mythology—medical, religious, social—may tell us, meat, red meat, has always been at the center of the human food experience. And that center holds, although it may be viewed either positively or negatively. Indeed, it often seems that our fascination with meat, our devotion to it, is sometimes more dramatically reflected in our violent reactions against it than in our everyday acceptance and consumption of it.

Consider, for example, the astonishingly wide range of taboos, social sanctions, and religious interdictions against meat and other animal foods. Hindus, whose vegetarianism can vary according to the orthodoxy of an individual's religious beliefs, forbid themselves absolutely the flesh of the cow, an animal that is utterly sacred, that may be neither killed nor consumed. This taboo is based on the sanctity of the animal and may at least in part reflect the fact that, in the peculiar ecology of Hindu India, the cow is more valuable alive than dead, its dung used for fuel and its milk for a variety of esteemed and valuable dairy products.

Buddhism, which also originated in India and had such a profound influence on so much of Southeast Asia and the Far East, also preaches vegetarianism, based not on the sanctity of any particular animal, but on the sanctity of all living things. Again, the degree of adherence to the ideals of the Buddha are varied and personal, ranging from a complete rejection of animal food of any kind (which might include the deliberate abstention from even a glass of water that could contain microscopic animal life) to the occasional observance of a nonmeat meal. Because in the Buddhist system all animal life is regarded as equally sacred, theoretically an ant or a worm is to be treated with as much reverence as a pig or a chicken.

Other cultures have other ways of dealing with the specialness of animal life. Many indigenous North American people were meat eaters but avoided certain animals because they were sacred or significant in tribal ritual. An individual or a clan might refrain from killing or eating a particular animal that functioned as its totem—that is, was thought to have some special relationship of ancestry or aid or protection. And even in cases in which the eating of those animals was permitted, it was usually done with special ritual observance, prayer, and thanks.

The other side of the coin that forbids the consumption of all meat or certain kinds of meat because it is sacred or special is the proscription of animal food because it is thought to be impure, unfit, or dangerous. The most comprehensive taboos of this sort occur in the Old Testament, with its lengthy and detailed strictures against a wide variety of animals. The animal prohibitions in Leviticus are much more extensive than most people realize because they have focused in more contemporary times primarily on pork and shellfish. The biblical list of animal prohibitions is a long one, and Islam, the other great religious system of the Middle East, draws heavily on it and condemns many of the same animals as unfit or defiling to observant Muslims.

Taboos or sanctions against animal foods are not necessarily limited to religious or ritual contexts. In our own culture red meat and derivative animal foods (eggs and dairy products) are widely regarded as dangerous substances, to be severely limited or completely avoided. Contemporary medical and nutritional thought may not seem to have the same power as a religious prohibition, but the effect is really much the same. If one eats certain foods, one takes a risk; the consumption of butter or eggs or bacon is seen as dangerous, damaging, and potentially lethal. And like the ancient and pervasive taboos that occur throughout history and across cultures, most modern sanctions center on meat and animal foods.

Curious, isn't it, that no culture seems to issue prohibitions against lima beans? Or forbids the reaping of rutabagas? Or incurs the Lord's wrath with a garnish of parsley? It is not that plant foods are disdained by their human consumers; indeed, some are worshiped, as Native Americans revere Mother Corn, the staple grain and the source of all life. It is not that we fail to value or enjoy the vegetable harvest or lack an appreciation of the truly great significance and pleasure of plant foods and products in our diet. But for most of us, no matter what the vagaries of history, geography, and culture have made of our cuisines, mere vegetables do not have the power to evoke the intense and profound emotions that meat and animal foods inevitably do. And whether our involvement with meat is a negative one (we fear it, we condemn it, we avoid it) or a positive one (we love it, we need it, we crave it), the response is almost always a stronger one than our response to, let us say, watercress.

The reasons for our intense reactions to animals are not very difficult to understand; animals are, after all, very much more like us than plants are. It is surely easier for us to identify with a mother bear nurturing her cubs than with a dandelion shedding its seeds upon the wind. But beyond the basic understanding that we ourselves are animals and are thereby connected to all other creatures is a more telling issue—and that is that almost any one of the myriad creatures that inhabit every corner of the earth is capable of providing humans with a more satisfying meal than any one of the far more numerous plants. However much we may fancy our avocados and Swiss chard, our sprouts and snap beans and sweet potatoes, from a purely nutritional point of view they can't hold a candle to a nice hunk of meat.

This may raise an eyebrow or two among those who have been brought up to believe that a pork chop represents instant death, or, conversely, that a few slivers of artfully placed zucchini and carrot are ample and adequate sustenance. But we must look at this business not from the point of view of our overfed and underexercised generation, but from the perspective of our ancient forebears, who spent the better part of their time and their energy searching for a decent meal, one that would sustain them in subsequent food forays and permit them as well to prosper and to propagate. In that context meat was the most efficient and effective nutritional package available.

The reason for meat's potency is quite simple: It contains all of the amino acids necessary for the growth, maintenance, and repair of the human body. Amino acids are the crucial building blocks of proteins; there are more than twenty that have been shown to be necessary for adequate human nutrition, and eight that are designated essential in that they must be provided by the diet in suitable amounts. Many foods, including plants, contain some or many amino acids; peas, beans, nuts, and cereal grains have a higher protein content than fruits or tubers or leafy greens. But no single plant or vegetable contains the full complement of essential amino acids that is found in meat or other animal products such as eggs or dairy foods.

In their long trek through history, humans have devised a number of strategies for dealing with the problem of obtaining sufficient protein in their diet. One of the most common, adopted by many groups of people throughout the world, is to combine plant or vegetable foods in such a way as to achieve a satisfactory balance of amino acids. Although no one plant food can provide adequate protein, two or more can do the job quite nicely, as long as they are eaten together at the same meal. So, for example, while kidney beans contain many of the essential amino acids, the few that they lack are conveniently supplied by corn, a grain that also happens to lack some of the acids found in the beans. Eaten together, corn and beans supply a suitable amount of all the essential amino acids, and these are known as complementary proteins.

Small wonder, then, that the indigenous people of the New World, from South America to Canada, have subsisted for many thousands of years on the combination of corn and beans, in such different culinary forms as tortillas and frijoles, succotash (stewed corn and lima beans), or baked beans and corn pone. Similarly, the people of the Orient combined the valuable soybean, in a variety of forms such as soy sauce, soy pastes, and soy curd (tofu), with rice or wheat. In India complementary proteins were provided by the pulses (split peas and lentils), eaten together with rice or wheat, and in the Middle East by the combination of chickpeas, fava beans, barley, and wheat. In all these diverse areas of the world, an apparent lack or scarcity of animal protein for many people was compensated for by the judicious combination of complementary plant proteins, and it was a solution that evolved independently in widely separated groups of people.

Another ancient solution to the protein problem developed along different lines, ones that led more directly to the context from which the cheeseburger would ultimately emerge. This was the domestication of animals, another widespread phenomenon involving different kinds of livestock in a variety of habitats throughout the world. It must have been apparent to many early people, hunting for their daily dinner, that the natural world was a frequently uncertain and variable source of animal food, that the fluctuations of climate and season could and often did lead to a disastrous lessening of animal resources. Certain areas throughout the globe provided animals that could easily be controlled or herded by man and that would breed successfully in captivity. The advantage of animal domestication is obvious: a reliable source of meat on the hoof. In return for the food, pasturage, and protection that humans provided, domesticated animals were to prove a dependable and ample supply of meat. And not insignificant from the gastronomic point of view, it was a supply of meat

that was more constant and dependable in its sensory qualities, for the animals' food was controlled and monitored by
man. An elk that has fed on pine needles has flesh that is
distinctly resinous in flavor and very different from the flavor
of an animal that has fed on acorns. And so began—for some
people, at any rate—a more successful way of obtaining protein, by controlling the forerunners of the animals that were
to become the modern world's major source of animal food
—the pig in China, the turkey in Mexico, sheep, goats, and
cattle in the Middle East and the highlands of Central Asia,
and in India a jungle fowl that would ultimately make the
fortune of one Colonel Sanders.

The advantages of animal domestication did not end with
meat itself. Only a creature with the superior brain of *Homo
sapiens* could have figured out that, as far as food is concerned, a live animal may be far more valuable than a dead
one. Chickens lay eggs, after all, and cows give milk, and
these products, as it turns out, are as satisfactory a source
of nourishment as the animal's flesh itself. A continuous
source of high-quality food that does not deplete the herd or
the flock is no small matter, and humans were quick to exploit
it—but of this, more in a later chapter.

So meat, as a highly satisfactory source of protein, a nearly
complete food in and of itself, has been coveted and sought
by man throughout history. The remains of charred bones
from ancient hearths, heaps of discarded mollusk shells from

riverbank and seacoast habitations, testify to the age-old, persistent search for meat in the human food saga. In addition to the more familiar fish, fowl, and flesh, an enormous variety of animal life was exploited, as it still is today in many parts of the world. Our finicky Western sensibilities may be offended by the notion of eating grubs, insects, worms, frogs, and snakes, but these creatures have provided good nourishment to a great many people throughout time.

Despite the wide variety of animal food that people have eaten in different places and under different circumstances, one kind has been consistently preferred and sought out over most others, and that is the flesh of other mammals. There are clear regional and cultural preferences regarding the particular variety of meat selected—pork in China, lamb in the Middle East, beef in England—but the taste for it appears to be nearly universal, an ancient and pervasive human hunger.

The reason for the extraordinarily wide appeal of this kind of meat, which we know as red meat, seems fairly clear: It contains not only a satisfactory balance of proteins, but, perhaps just as important, a good dose of animal fat. More than fish, shellfish, or poultry, mammal flesh provides a high percentage of fat, some of which surrounds the muscle tissue and some of which is marbleized within it. And it is this rich protein-fat package that is of such compelling appeal to the human consumer.

And here, let's be clear what we mean by "red meat," for

it is a term that has been somewhat misunderstood in the current health and nutrition context. Red meat refers to the flesh of mammals that is red, reddish brown, or reddish purple in color, and that can be distinguished from flesh that is white or creamy in color. Beef and lamb are clearly red meats, while veal and rabbit are white meats; the white meat category has been generalized to include the flesh of poultry and fish as well. Red meats generally contain a much heavier load of saturated fats than white meats and therefore have been implicated as a significant dietary factor in the development of coronary artery disease and elevated cholesterol levels. It is important to note, however, that the color of meat is not necessarily a reliable indicator of the fat content. The red color is caused by a blood pigment that is not always correlated with the fattiness. Venison is red, for example, but like many other game meats has much less fat than domesticated red meats; pork is white but contains much the same saturated fat as beef or lamb.

It is clear that people in a wide variety of cultures and habitats have placed a heavier significance on red meat than on most other foods. The inexorable push throughout human history seems to have been to get hold of as much of that good stuff as possible, for the protein-fat package is one of the most effective and efficient forms of nourishment ever discovered. We can readily appreciate the necessity of adequate proteins in the diet, essential ingredients in the growth, maintenance, and repair of body tissues and vital organs. But fat? How are we, who have been so strongly conditioned by contemporary mythology to think of fat as a dirty word, to understand the meaning and the value of fat in the larger picture, in the longer view? If fat is so bad for us, why do we want it so much and why has the quest for it been so clearly a part of our species' history?

Dietary fat serves much the same function as carbohydrate; it is used by the body as a source of energy, as the fuel that drives all the many parts of this complex living machine. From the pumping of the blood to the blinking of the eyes to the flexing of the knees, from the minute to the gross, all the actions and movements of the myriad components of the human body are fueled, kept going, by the food we eat, primarily in the form of carbohydrates (sugars and starches) and fats. The only difference between carbohydrates and fats, in terms of their function, is the rate at which they are converted into energy. Carbohydrates are an immediate and rapid source of fuel, while the more concentrated fats are stored in the body as a long-term, slowly released form of energy. For a creature who evolved initially as a hunter and forager, whose food resources were surely variable and inconstant, the advantages of dietary fat are clear: Fat in the body is like money in the bank, a hedge today against scarcity and deprivation in the weeks and months ahead. The energy from a meal of roots and berries is quickly used up, but the energy from the tail of a fat sheep will stick with you to be used in times of need. Fat performs other essential functions as well. It provides the body with insulation and padding (a fact of which we are only too well aware when the bathing suit season rolls around), plays an important role in metabolism, and is a carrier for two essential vitamins, A and D.

So from the larger human perspective (no pun intended), fat is a very desirable and a very necessary food substance. And it is clear that, as with protein, human interest in fat focuses on its animal rather than its plant sources. For fat is found in vegetable as well as animal foods, in the form of vegetable oils. These oils are concentrated primarily in the seed parts of the plant, for the seed is the propagative agent and it too requires stored reserves of energy for its reproductive purposes. All seeds, whether nuts or legumes or grains, contain variable amounts of vegetable oil, and they are as valuable a source of dietary fat as animal foods. The problem initially was that you would have had to eat an awful lot of seeds to get as much oil as you could get in a couple of good bites of animal fat; either that or you would have had to spend a great deal of time and energy pressing the oil from the seeds, assuming that you had a large enough supply of them to make such an enterprise worthwhile.

The vegetable oil alternative to animal fat is an option that was selected by many cultures throughout the world—oil from olives in the Near East and the Mediterranean, oil from soybeans and sesame seeds in Asia, and, after the discovery of the New World, oil from corn and peanuts and sunflower seeds. From the long view of human history, they are relatively recent developments. All are predicated on the domestication of certain seed crops in order to ensure an adequate supply, and on the development of a technology for the pressing or extraction of the oil. From the point of view of simple energy expenditure, a nice hunk of meat encased in or marbleized with fat may be a lot easier and more efficient than growing and gathering seeds and then expressing their oil.

It is not surprising, therefore, that many of our traditions reflect our involvement and fascination with animals and animal fat. Hear, for example, the sonorous proclamation of the Old Testament, so rich a storehouse for subsequent centuries of Western sensibilities, on the matter of animal sacrifice:

> And the priest shall burn them on the altar as food offered by fire for a pleasing odor. All fat is the Lord's. It shall be a perpetual statute throughout your generations, in all your dwelling places, that you eat neither fat nor blood.
>
> (Leviticus 3: 16,17)

In ancient Judaism fat, like blood, was special and sacred to the Lord, His portion of the peace offering, while the rest of the roasted sacrificial animal was consumed in a communion meal by the priests and the congregation. The practice of separating and sanctifying animal fat declined in Judaic tradition after the destruction of the Temple and the subsequent cessation of animal sacrifice as a part of ritual observance, while the sanction against blood remains in effect to this day for observant Jews. But the notion that fat was special and desirable was evident not only in the ancient Middle East but also in other places and more remote periods of human history.

The archaeological record provides evidence that is at least four hundred thousand years old. In the Choukoutien caves outside of Beijing, China, there were discovered the hearths of *Homo erectus*, a forerunner of *Homo sapiens*. Among the charred remains left by Peking man were bones that had been carefully split so that the marrow could be extracted. Yellow marrow, found in the long bones—arms and legs—of mammals, is a rich substance, ninety-five percent fat, that humans have long coveted as a great delicacy; we perpetuate that experience today when we indulge in the savory delight of osso buco. Peking man seems unfortunately to have preferred his neighbors' shanks to veal, for the ancient marrow bones were unmistakably human, and they had apparently been roasted, not braised.

And while we're on the subject of cannibalism and fat, there is another scenario to consider. The Aztecs of pre-

Columbian Mexico practiced a religion in which human sacrifice was a focal ritual. Thousands of victims were captured and fattened as sacrificial offerings to an unusually bloodthirsty set of gods; while the still-beating heart and accompanying rush of blood were given in sacrifice, the rest of the victim's body was consumed by the priests and the other privileged members of the society. Some modern anthropologists have speculated that this intense level of blood sacrifice and cannibalism may have had more to do with ecology than theology; a lack of dietary fat and the absence of the common domesticated animals—pigs, cows, sheep, goats—in pre-Columbian Mexico encouraged the hunting and herding of two-footed animals, whose flesh was fine and fat.

Clearly, the Aztec example, if valid, is an extreme case; nonetheless, many traditional cultures provide evidence for the widespread human taste for fat. In the Middle East and Mongolia the tail portion of the sheep, with its large deposits of fat, has always been a favored delicacy, while in North America the tail of the beaver was esteemed for exactly the same reason. Among many Native Americans the bear was a choice game animal because of its sweet and abundant fat, used not only to soften and moisturize peoples' hair and skin but also to enrich their bean dishes. When European colonists arrived in the New World, they substituted their preferred pig fat for the bear fat, a tradition that remains viable today in the popular dish of baked beans.

If we have, throughout our history, so greatly valued fat, we have chosen for the most part to consume it not by itself but along with its companion, animal flesh. (The clear exception to this general rule is the Arctic Eskimo, who subsisted on a diet extraordinarily rich in fat, primarily in the form of seal blubber. The traditional Eskimo, however, inhabited an environment that is so extreme in terms of climate and resources that almost no culinary or nutritional generalization can apply.) But as is so often the case with our eccentric species, it seems unlikely that nutritional concerns alone can account for the fascination with flesh and fat. The fact is, the flesh-fat package appeals to human carnivores in ways beyond the experience or understanding of other carnivores for whom the nutritional benefits may be exactly the same. The difference is quite simply that humans cook their meat, and it is this, the cooking process—unique to our kind—that expanded the eating of meat from the merely nutritious to the delightfully delicious, that forever shifted the human experience of food from simple satiation to the full-blown complexities of cuisine.

What is it exactly, then, that happens to meat and fat when they are cooked together that can account for this marvelous enlargement of sensibilities, for the explosion of the aesthetic? It is, in the simplest terms, the browning of meat and the liquefaction of fat, occurring together and simultaneously. Not such a big deal, one might think, but from the long perspective it was one of those discoveries or happenings that would change us all forever. How did it happen? We can only speculate, for there are no written records, no Ur-recipes carved into ancient rocks. It must have happened a thousand different times in a thousand different places, but it was of no significance whatsoever until a creature came along who had a brain capable of understanding and appreciating the event and the motivation and capability to reproduce it.

Imagine it thus: A small band of two-footed upright creatures trudges across the savanna, skirting a still-smoldering grass fire started by a lightning strike. Suddenly there is a shift in the wind and the leader of the group, an elderly female perhaps thirty years old, stops and sniffs the air. Motioning the band to stop, she turns toward the burning grassland and, with great caution and quivering nostrils, searches for the source of the unknown odor, unfamiliar yet tantalizingly agreeable. And there it is—a crippled gazelle, unable to outrun the rapidly sweeping fire, has been slowly roasting on the burning stubble, still too hot for the vultures circling overhead. Coming closer, the female pokes at the animal with a stick, and as the pleasant aroma intensifies, she motions for the others to pull the carcass from the burning grass. Their quarry secure on cool ground, the group squats to observe and to smell the wonderful odor; some of them lick the juices from their burning fingers. Sniffing their hands and chattering with mounting excitement, they watch their leader hack off a chunk of meat, bring it to her nose, then take a lick and a tentative bite. She smiles and nods, then takes another nibble, a small one, because many of her teeth are missing and she cannot chew very well. But this is good stuff! The smell of it is irresistible, the taste of it no less so. The skin is browned and crispy, the warm meat running with juice and fat, far more tender and tasty than anything else she has ever put into her mouth. And it is just this scenario—romantic perhaps, but not improbable—that is the origin of our beloved burger.

What happens when meat is grilled or roasted—that is, when it is exposed to heat with air present as opposed to heating it in liquid—is a complex set of events that produces a characteristic odor and flavor. The browning of the meat that occurs when certain amino acids and sugars are subject to dry heat is known as the Maillard effect, and it is this process that results in the enticing aroma and "meaty" flavor that is so universally attractive. As the meat cooks, the fat within and around it melts, bathing the meat with many flavor compounds, lubricating the flesh, and making it juicy and glistening. The liquefied fat is itself the source of much flavor and aroma, in addition to the succulence and gratifying mouth feel it provides. Much later in history, people would discover that cooking food in fat or oil produced many of the same desirable effects as dry heat—browning, carmelization of sugars, production of additional flavor compounds—and would then use frying or sautéeing for those purely gastronomic ends. It is for this very simple reason that we generally brown meat, onions, carrots, and so on in fat or oil before we cook them in liquid; the browning produces additional flavor that would not otherwise be available. It is this process and the product he termed "osmazone" that Brillat-Savarin, the nineteenth-century author of the book *The Physiology of Taste*, stipulated as necessary to the making of a good soup; "osmazone," he said, "is derived, above all, from full-grown animals with dark reddish flesh, such as are called 'meaty.' . . . When it has passed into a state resembling caramel it forms the browning of meat, as well as the crisp-brown of roast-meat; finally, from it the odour of venison and game arise."

The aroma of roasted meat is for humans a clear and crucial precursor to the flavor and the other mouth experiences that occur when we actually eat roasted meat. Why this olfactory prelude—a kind of aromatic foreplay—to actual consumption is so important to us may be due in part to the fact that as a species we have lost much of the smelling ability of other animals, particularly of carnivores like wolves or hyenas, who can scent prey living or dead from great distances. Our sniffers are not particularly sensitive, and the accidental discovery of cooking by fire may have acted as a pleasurable stimulant to our underdeveloped noses. Small wonder, then, that roasted meat is so pervasive a sacrificial offering to our gods; the delicious aroma, invisible yet powerful, rises toward the heavens. It is, as the Old Testament tells us, "an odor that is pleasing to the Lord."

If roasting meat perked up our nasal sensibilities, it seems in a larger way to have awakened the aesthetic urge so characteristic of our species, the gastronomic imperative that compels us to experience the pleasure, the joy, of eating, quite apart from its nutritive function. For after all, from a purely functional point of view, we can be as successfully nourished with raw meat as with cooked, but we inevitably choose, except in the direst circumstances, to endure the delay that cooking requires in order to provide ourselves with a finished product that we regard as clearly superior. It is a product that transcends nourishment and transports us to realms of experience unknown to any other creature. Surely no one has described that experience more eloquently than the nineteenth-century essayist Charles Lamb in "A Dissertation Upon Roast Pig":

He must be roasted. I am not ignorant that our ancestors ate them seethed, or boiled—but what a sacrifice of the exterior tegument!

There is no flavor comparable, I will contend, to that of the crisp, tawny, well-watched, not over-roasted *crackling,* as it is well called—the very teeth are invited to their share of the pleasure at this banquet in overcoming the coy, brittle resistance—with the adhesive oleaginous—O call it not fat—but an undefinable sweetness growing up to it—the tender blossoming of fat—fat cropped in the bud—taken in the shoot—in the first innocence—the cream and quintessence of the child-pig's yet pure food—the lean, no lean, but a kind of animal manna—or, rather, fat and lean (if it must be so) blended and running into each other, that both together make but one ambrosian result, or common substance.

If cooked or roasted meat appealed to our noses and our taste buds, it was attractive as well for the textural experiences it offered, as Lamb's tribute so movingly describes. Certainly for the very earliest consumers the most obvious and the most welcome change between raw and cooked meat would have been its increased tenderness, for cooking breaks down the connective fibers in flesh, making it easier to chew and easier to swallow. For humans this was an enormous advantage; we do not possess the specialized equipment of the true carnivore—sharp teeth that can rip and tear raw flesh and digestive systems capable of processing large hunks of meat. And cooked meat was further tenderized by the liquefied fat marbleized within and surrounding the muscle tissue.

For those of us who have grown up with fluoride toothpaste, orthodontia, and semiannual dental checkups as a routine and expected part of life, it is hard to estimate how important tender, chewable food must have been to our ancestors. For as both the archaeological and historical records indicate, teeth are a very crucial but vulnerable part of our anatomy, subject to wear and tear, infection, cavities, breakage, and loss. The increased tenderness of meat that cooking provided was a great leap forward for all humans, but particularly for those whose chewing apparatus was somehow compromised. (Even today it is estimated that dental problems are the major barrier to good nutrition in the elderly.) In addition to the cooking process itself, early people would no doubt have realized that cutting or chopping or pounding the meat into smaller and smaller pieces would also be of great value for those who could not chew too well.

Tradition has it that ground meat was invented by people from Central Asia, fierce horsemen whom history records by the names of Mongols, Huns, Scythians, and Tartars. It is the last of these who have immortalized the legend by giving their name to the concoction of seasoned ground raw meat, steak tartare. These warriors, it is said, stashed slabs of meat under their saddles as they dashed about the world on their ponies, pillaging, looting, and conquering. After a long day's ride the meat was pounded to a pulp and seasoned to boot with a hefty dose of saddle oil, not to mention a soupçon of sweat from the horse's rump!

Despite this fetching scenario, it is far more likely that the technique of reducing meat to smaller and smaller particles developed much earlier in our history as a thoughtful and practical response to dental problems and the needs of the very young and the very old. Indeed, in many traditional cultures women with strong teeth frequently masticate meat to a paste and then feed it to their infants and to the elderly. And of course the frugal impulse to utilize every edible scrap of meat from a butchered animal resulted throughout the centuries in the development of such products as sausages, hashes, croquettes, and the like.

Finely particulated meat, ground or shredded or minced or chopped, has always been very appealing because it is so easy. It offers the full nutritional and sensory experience of meat to everyone—the young, the old, the toothless, and the tired. In addition to easy chewing, ground meat has another advantage, and that is that the meat and the fat are uniformly distributed throughout the mass, making each bite equally juicy and equally tender. And with the development of technology, ground meat became easier and easier to produce, starting with rocks for pounding, wooden mallets, then proceeding through Mongol saddles, metal choppers, hand grinders, and finally to the great automated commercial grinders of the modern meat processor.

No doubt there have been through the ages an infinite variety of burgerlike products, ground or pounded meat molded on skewers or spits, slapped on grills, griddles, and frying pans. Consider, for example, this remarkably modern-sounding recipe, a two-thousand-year-old preparation from an ancient Chinese text, the *Li chi*:

> To make the grill, they beat the beef and removed the skinny parts. They then laid it on a frame of reeds, sprinkled on it pieces of cinnamon and ginger, and added salt.

And, no doubt, any number of different meats was used—think of the ground lamb kabobs of the Middle East, the pork sausages of Europe, the pemmicans of North America, even the mooseburgers of modern-day Alaska. But *the* burger, the one recognized and loved throughout the world, is made of beef. Why beef? Why not lamb or pork or moose or water buffalo? The reasons are many and complex, but there is a sense one gets of the inevitability of beef in the contemporary experience, as though our long quest through history was guided by an urge finally voiced by an old lady in a TV commercial. "WHERE'S THE *BEEF?*" she growled, and her voice spoke for millennia of hungry seekers. It is a hunger that may well prove to be destructive to ourselves and the planet we inhabit—and the two are inseparable. But it is a road already taken, and we must try to understand it.

Cattle were first domesticated in the Near East some seven thousand to eight thousand years ago, spreading east to Asia and India and west to Europe and the Mediterranean. Beef was eaten by many people throughout the world, but never on a wide scale. Cows are expensive; they require vast acreage to provide adequate grazing. In traditional cultures cows are generally more valuable alive than dead, providing milk, fuel from their dung, and a source of wealth for barter or trade. In many herding societies, like the Masai of East Africa, meat from cattle is consumed only for ceremonial occasions or when the animals die a natural death; the ordinary diet is provided by the live animal in the form of milk and blood, which is skillfully drawn from the veins without harm to the cows.

So although beef has been widely known and esteemed across the globe, it has not been very heavily exploited as human food, like pigs or chickens, for example, which are cheaper and easier to keep. But beef has long been the meat of choice in Western Europe. The great chef Carême, acknowledged to be the founding father of La Grande Cuisine Française, the great tradition of classic French cooking as we understand it today, proclaimed that "beef is the soul of cooking." And no wonder. The French have long had a jealous proprietary interest in their beloved *bifteck;* and the bones of beef, boiled down into precious concentrated essences, *glaces de viande,* form the basis of the great classic sauces.

The passion of the English for their roast beef is legendary, celebrated in prose and verse by dozens of writers from

Shakespeare to Henry Fielding to Samuel Johnson. King Henry II was so enamored of a prime steak that he knighted it, dubbing it Sir Loin, and we have shared his passion and the name ever since. Beef was so highly valued no doubt in part because it was an expensive and luxurious food, but it was appreciated primarily because it possessed the choicest qualities of meat and meatiness—an exemplary flavor that was neither too bland nor too strong or gamey, an attractive red or sanguine juiciness (for unlike most other meats it was often eaten rare), and a perception that it enriched and empowered all who partook of its virtues. And domestic beef was generously marbled with fat, providing an unparalleled flavor and tenderness.

Despite its appeal, beef remained only an occasional food for the privileged. Common folk in Europe nourished themselves with grains and beans, bread and gruel, their protein needs supplemented by occasional dairy products and the cheaper, more easily available fish, poultry, and smoked or salted pork. Fresh red meat, and particularly domesticated beef, did not become a food for the common man until it was established in that mecca for the common man, the New World.

Columbus's landing in the Bahamas in 1492 was a jumpstart for the development of the cheeseburger, for the Americas, both North and South, contained vast virgin prairies and plains, a rich and seemingly limitless source of pasturage for domesticated cattle. The incoming settlers, primarily Western Europeans with an already established taste for beef, were quick to exploit the wondrous resources of their new homeland. Cattle raising became big business and beef was produced on a grand scale unprecedented in human history. For the first time, with an unparalleled scope, the most esteemed of red meats became the cheap and plentiful food of the masses. It is truly remarkable that in only a few short centuries this universally esteemed livestock—whether as the sacred cow of a religious belief system or as the flesh-and-bones foundation of a culinary enterprise, valued and craved for its expense and luxury—would become the daily indulgence of the most ordinary folk, yet no less admired because of its sudden availability.

The beef of the Americas is not only cheap and plentiful, but it is also by most accounts the best beef in the world—except, perhaps, for such an exotic anomaly as the beer-fed, hand-massaged Kobe beef of the Japanese. But quality, surely, is not an important issue for the burger, which does not claim to provide the same experience as that of a prime steak or a filet mignon or a slab of aged prime rib. The meaning of the burger is as a kind of common denominator of the beef experience, with all the flavor, aroma, tenderness, and juiciness in a cheap and accessible form. The meatiness, the beefiness, the succulence of the fat are all there in that unassuming little patty. For perhaps the first time ever, the hunger for all that beef is, for all that beef represents, can easily be satisfied, is available to almost anyone—and it is perfectly clear that almost everyone wants it. It provides a genuine fulfillment of that atavistic craving in all of us for tender roasted meat running with fat and juice, a hunger that seems to have been a common part of our shared experience as human beings.

Two

THE BUN

*I*n terms of sheer visual impact the bun is the largest and most obvious component of the cheeseburger platter. Round, puffed, a tempting golden brown with an eye-catching sprinkle of sesame seeds, it is the focus, the center, the treasure chest that holds the precious burger with its attendant savories. The bun is parted slightly to reveal some, but not all, of its juicy cargo, offering a tantalizing glimpse of anticipated delights and hidden surprises. But the bun itself is all there, out in the open, for our immediate acknowledgment, soft yet sturdy, reliable, self-confident. It does not evoke excitement or anticipatory salivation, like the burger itself, but functions rather as the housing, the essential structure that holds everything together.

And that is as it should be, for the bun is bread, and it is bread that has nourished and sustained us throughout our history. We may always have craved the meat, the burger, but we frequently couldn't get it or weren't permitted to eat it, and when we were unable to satisfy our lust for flesh, we turned to the perhaps less stimulating but more dependable grains to quiet our hunger and fill our bellies.

Grains are seeds, the seeds of different grass plants that grow in a variety of habitats throughout the globe. Of the many thousands of grasses only a small number have proved to be of enduring value as food to humans, and these are known as the cereal grains. The name comes from Ceres, the Roman goddess of vegetation, who was herself but one of many incarnations of an earlier deity, the Earth Mother, who nurtured her children with the fruits of the earth. Ceres gave her name to Cerealia, a spring festival that celebrated the new growth of all vegetables; the name for us has come to mean more specifically the grain foods—flaked, popped, crisped, shredded—that form the first meal of the day, the meal with which we break our fast of the night.

The cereal grains are a valuable food because they contain a great many of the nutrients that humans need to nourish themselves satisfactorily. They are composed largely of starch cells, which are a source of carbohydrate, and an inner germ, which contains variable amounts of both protein and vegetable oil. The carbohydrate content of most grains is about seventy to eighty percent, while the protein content varies from between five and about sixteen percent. The outer layer, or bran, contains valuable dietary fiber as well as some other important nutrients, certain vitamins and minerals. The cereal grains are in general a rich source of the B-complex vitamins—including thiamine, niacin, and riboflavin—as well as the minerals iron and calcium. Whole grains are those whose outer bran layers or inner germ portions have not been removed in the milling process; refined grains are those that have had some portion of the kernel removed—the outer bran in white rice and white wheat flour, the germ in degerminated cornmeal. Enriched grains or grain products are those that have had some of the removed nutrients restored in the manufacturing process.

Because the cereal grains are such a valuable source of nutrients, they were likely used as food from the earliest periods of our history. But these grass seeds are relatively small and were probably smaller still in their wild state; they likely did not form a significant part of the human diet until they were deliberately cultivated, although it is certainly possible that true agriculture was preceded by intermediary stages in which people sought out or camped near productive stands of wild grain. The invention of agriculture, the cultivation of the cereal grains, is thought to have occurred some ten thousand years ago in the Near and Middle East with the deliberate planting and harvesting of wheat and barley. Parallel inventions occurred with different grains in different parts of the world—rice in Southeast Asia and India, millet in Africa, maize in the Americas, and later, rye and oats in Central and Northern Europe. In all these cases, as with the domestication of animals, there was a two-way exchange between humans and their crops. The farmer planted, tended, weeded, and watered, selecting for larger, sturdier, more productive varieties, and received in return an abundant, reliable supply of nourishing food. The cultivation of the cereal grains—what has been aptly called the agricultural revolution—was a clear turning point in human history, changing us from nomadic foragers into acquisitive hoarders and squatters, and changing forever what we ate and how we cooked it.

Because the cereal grains are basically hard and dry, they are of little value as human food until they have been processed in some manner. There are several basic ways that people discovered to deal with their grain foods, and those practices remain as viable today as they were in the very beginning. The first of the techniques is the simplest—whole unprocessed grains cooked in water until they absorb the liquid, swell, and become soft. The way we cook rice today is no different from the way it was cooked in China four thousand years ago. This treatment of the cereal grains led to a whole complex of dishes with which the world has long been familiar: soups, porridges, gruels, pilafs. Whether the dish is in the form of an oatmeal porridge, a barley soup, or a rice congee, it is structurally the same thing—a whole grain cooked in liquid until it becomes a soft, palatable, and rib-sticking bowl of nourishment, easy to eat and easy to digest.

The practice of softening or cooking grains in water led inevitably, and no doubt very quickly, to another ancient and

well-loved product, beer; wherever in the world people cultivated cereal grains, they developed an alcoholic beverage or
beer made from that grain. Evidence of beer making from
five thousand years ago has been discovered in ancient tombs
of Egypt and Mesopotamia, and the widespread practice suggests that the tradition is far more venerable than that. And
why not? Beer is not only calorically rich but provides its
consumer with a pleasant high, a nourishing, thirst-quenching,
feel-good experience.

The reason for the inevitable association of beer with grain
cookery is clear: Grains left to soak in water for a long
enough time at the right temperature become soft and sprout,
a process known as "malting." Malting produces enzymes
that break down the grains' starch molecules into less complex
sugars; these sugars are then digested by yeasts, microscopic
fungi abundant in the natural environment. The yeasts con-
vert the sugars into carbon dioxide and alcohol—the process
of fermentation—and a bubbly, mildly alcoholic beverage is
the result.

The second great tradition of grain cookery involved grinding, pounding, or milling the uncooked grains into a dry meal
or flour. The flour would then be mixed with liquid, usually
water, to form some sort of batter or dough. This dough
could then be treated in a couple of basic ways to produce
the large variety of milled grain products that are such an
important part of the world's table. First, pieces of the dough

can be cooked in liquid. Pinched, rolled, stretched, shaped, or cut into a variety of shapes and sizes, the dough becomes what we know as dumplings, noodles, or pasta, and the potential for variation is seemingly endless. The contemporary Italian inventory of pasta is an eye-opening demonstration of human ingenuity and playfulness in dealing with the simple technique of boiling pieces of dough in water: from priests' hats, *cappelli di prete;* to little butterflies or bows, *farfellette;* to snails, *lumache;* to grooved electric wire, *elettrici rigati;* not to mention all the noodles, round and flat, thick and thin, the tubes, ribbons, twists, and dumplings—an astonishing adventure in texture and visual appeal.

Most of our modern noodles and pastas are made of finely milled white wheat flour, which provides an elastic, easily worked dough, a smooth, firm texture, and an appealing white or creamy color. But there are products that have traditionally been made from a number of different milled grains; the Orient has an extensive repertoire of goods made from rice flour—both noodles, frequently called "rice sticks," and rice "paper" wrappings for rolled or filled snacks. The Hopi people of the American Southwest make dumplings from their traditional blue cornmeal; called "blue marbles," they add substance and variety to soups and stews. The technique of grinding grains into flour or meal, then mixing the flour with water to form a dough that is then cooked in liquid, is an

ancient one and a one-step advance in complexity from the
simple cooking of whole grains in water.

The other great tradition of cooking with ground cereal
grains mixed with water is one that uses dry heat rather than
liquid to cook the dough, and that, of course, is the tradition
that leads directly to our hamburger bun. Bread, the food
that has so long and so well sustained so many of our kind
—the staff of life that is synonymous with nourishment, with
life itself—symbolizes, in Western mythology at least, the shift
from natural unprocessed food to the culturally transformed
products of human cuisine. The essence of humanness is to
process food, to manipulate it, to change it from its raw
pristine state into something other. And of those culturally
created foods, bread has always been one of the most basic
and most pervasive.

The bread of our earliest ancestors must have been tough
and gritty stuff indeed. It was made of dry grains ground or
pounded by hand with stones on rocks specially selected or
shaped for the purpose, known as querns in the Old World
and metates in the New. The flour or meal would no doubt
have been imperfectly ground, with bits of whole grains and
chaff, and some gritty residue from the grinding stones. This
uneven mixture, mixed with water and then cooked in the
ashes of the hearth fire, would not have been very palatable
by modern standards, but it provided a nourishing and sat-

isfying meal, though it was no doubt very hard on the teeth. Evidence for the grinding of seeds and grains occurs throughout the world, ancient testimony of the nearly universal human need to supplement scarce animal resources with processed plant foods that provide adequate nourishment. It would not have been long before people discovered that baking these coarse cakes on a clean stone surface placed in or over the coals would at least eliminate the taste of ashes and the carbonization that occurred when the bread was cooked directly in the ashes, and so would have been born the griddle or cooking stone on which so many flat breads are still baked today. The *comal* of Mexico is made of metal nowadays, but before metal it was made of pottery and before pottery it was made of stone; whatever the material, the concept is the same, and it is one that developed worldwide. The modern tortilla, the pita of the Middle East, the chapati of India, and the injera of Ethiopia are simply more highly processed versions of their ancient forms—flat unleavened cakes of ground grains such as barley, wheat, millet, or maize, cooked with dry heat on flat griddles.

So we have the earliest form of bread, flat chewy dry cakes or loaves that seem very different from our modern breads. What changed primarily throughout history are the sensory attributes—the flavor, color, and texture—of the product, and this was due to two innovations. The first was very likely an accidental discovery, the second an ongoing deliberate attempt to change existing breads into something different and presumably better.

The accidental discovery was that of leavening bread dough to produce a loaf that was lighter, fluffier, and softer than the familiar unleavened flat breads. The discovery seems to have occurred in Egypt some four thousand to five thousand years ago. Egypt was of course the home of one of the great civilizations of the ancient world, a civilization built on the cultivation of barley and wheat, and of a particular variety of wheat known as hard or bread wheat.

Not all milled grains are capable of being leavened; wheat differs significantly from other cereals because it contains varying amounts of gluten, a protein that is capable of great expansion. Hard or bread wheat contains larger chunks of gluten than the other varieties and therefore provides a substance that can be leavened or raised. The ground bread flour, mixed with water and left to stand at the proper temperature, will expand because of the fermentative action of ever-present yeast organisms. Feeding on the natural sugars in the grain, the yeasts produce carbon dioxide, which is trapped as bubbles in the expanding gluten particles, thus producing a puffed and airy structure in the baked loaf.

The appropriate ingredients and circumstances seem to have come together in ancient Egypt, and the original scenario is not hard to imagine. The village baker, an enterprising young man named Abdoul, is mixing up a batch of dough for the weekly bread baking. Just as he finishes shaping his flat round loaves, the alarm sounds and Abdoul rushes off with the other men to defend the town against a horde of raiding barbarians. Returning some hours later, he is horrified to discover that his lovely little flat loaves have mysteriously puffed into large round balls. But the oven is still hot and so, checking over his shoulder to make sure no one is watching, he furtively slips one of the balls into the oven and sits back on his heels to see what will happen. Half an hour later he fishes out the loaf, now golden brown and emitting a fragrant, yeasty aroma. He breaks open the loaf and stares in amazement at the light, spongy texture; an experimental nibble makes his head spin. The tender soft bread with its crunchy golden crust is truly a food for the gods.

Abdoul knows a good thing when he sees it; he quickly places all the other dough balls into the oven, keeping out only one to fool around with. He pokes it, prods it, rolls it around in his hands, and is astonished to find that it is reduced to its original flat state and that no amount of pushing or squeezing can reproduce that wondrous puffed condition. He tosses it aside, only to discover the next morning that it has risen once again and, when baked, produces an even lighter and tenderer loaf. With his experimental nature he will soon realize that a bit of the leavened dough, when added to a new batch of dough, will hasten and intensify the leavening process, resulting in breads that are even more flavorful and tender.

Abdoul's great invention, which he calls "wonder" bread, is an instant success, and his fame spreads far and wide. On baking day the village virgins gather at the bakery to ogle and flirt and poke the rising bread with suggestive giggles. The James Beard Foundation honors Abdoul as the Rising Young Baker of the Middle Kingdom. And a whole generation of Pharaonic hippies will grow up on the slogan "Raise bread, not pyramids!"

That leavened bread was an Egyptian invention or discovery makes the Jewish matzo an even more meaningful food. The celebration of Passover, which commemorates the exodus of the Jews from bondage in Egypt, features among many ritually significant foods the matzo, a modern version of ancient unleavened bread. In their haste to leave Egypt the Jews did not have time to leaven their dough, and took as sustenance for the journey to the promised land the old quickly cooked flat bread. Haste may have been the primary motivation for rejecting leavened bread at that point, but that it was an Egyptian food could hardly have been unimportant.

The ingeniousness of Abdoul notwithstanding, it is still a long time and many miles to go before we get to our hamburger bun, and the reason is quite simply that wheat was not a universally grown grain and remained for many centuries an expensive luxury. Imperial Rome used its conquered colonies in the Near East and North Africa as a bread basket to supply the coveted wheat for bread to fill the greedy mouths of the Roman elite. Common people continued to nourish themselves with the cheaper whole-grain porridges and coarse unleavened grain cakes, but everyone, it seems, aspired to the fine leavened wheat bread with its spongy soft texture and light color.

Which brings us to the second innovation in the history of bread production, one that seems to have gone hand in hand with the accidental discovery of leavening. This is the deliberate pursuit of light, white, soft, refined breads or, in other words, the intensification of all the sensory attributes produced by the fermentive action of yeast on wheat dough. For while wheat, and more specifically bread wheat, was the only grain that could be satisfactorily leavened, it was discovered that the finer the wheat was milled, the finer and whiter the bread would be. The grain itself was expensive and the additional processes necessary to refine it made it even more so—and there is nothing like costliness and rarity to give food a special panache.

Lightness, whiteness, fineness, and tenderness became hallmarks for the best in bread, equated not only with aesthetic values and social prestige but with nutritional value as well. A hygienist quoted by the Greek writer Athenaeus in the third century A.D. declared: "Bread made of wheat, as compared with that made of barley, is more nourishing, more digestible, and in every way superior. In order of merit, the bread made from refined flour comes first, after that the bread of ordinary wheat, and then the unbolted, made of flour that has not been sifted." That pronouncement is of course exactly opposite to the contemporary view, which holds that less refined, whole-grain flour is far superior nutritionally to flour that is highly refined.

For whatever the reasons—social, economic, gastronomic —light, refined, leavened bread continued to be esteemed in Europe, and most certainly in England, which would come to be the source of so much subsequent American tradition. Medieval England produced many different kinds of bread, but they could be described by two basic categories. The lowliest, called *cheate,* was made of coarsely ground mixtures of whole grains—wheat, barley, rye, oats—and was the bread eaten by the poorest and lowest on the social scale. The best bread was called *manchet,* made of highly refined wheat flour. William Harrison, a contemporary of Shakespeare, wrote, "We have sundry sorts brought to the table, whereof the first and most excellent is manchet, which we commonly call white bread."

White bread! The stuff of the American dream, airy, soft, light, bland, and fluffy, the perfection of mankind's long experiment with the cereal grains, finally the beloved staple of the commonest of the common folk. For it was in America that wheat would first be grown on a grand scale and industrial equipment designed to refine or "bolt" the wheat into the finest, whitest flour ever known. And if milling didn't get it white enough, the flour was lightened with chemical bleaches. That the bread made from this highly processed flour was not very valuable nutritionally was quickly remedied: Vitamins and minerals lost in the milling process were replaced in the manufacture, and commercial white breads were further enriched with the addition of shortening (fats), milk products, and eggs. These ingredients added not only nutrients (and of course a great many more calories), but further enhanced those qualities of white bread that we have always esteemed—softness, smoothness, and tenderness.

Lightness or whiteness are valued qualities that are not limited to bread alone. Historically, refined sugar, with its pure white crystals and bland sweet flavor, has been more preferred than its unrefined precursors, with their dark brown color and more distinctive flavor. The people of the Orient have long valued hulled and polished white rice, even though the removal of the husk or bran results in a product that is far less nutritionally useful. (The issue of husked rice is a complicated one, because husked rice is less susceptible to fungal infection than unhusked rice; the preference for white rice may at least in part reflect an initial adaptive response to a food that could be successfully stored for longer periods of time.) A desire for whiteness or lightness in certain foods is widespread, but it is by no means universal. Most of us prefer light-colored, white- or creamy-fleshed potatoes, but the native people of the Andes, where the potato originated, have long cultivated many kinds and colors, including black- and purple-fleshed varieties. Native Americans still value many colors of corn, including black, blue, red, and speckled, but European immigrants to the New World stuck exclusively to the white and yellow varieties, with their less intense color and less pronounced flavor.

Still, where bread is concerned, the thrust throughout history has been quite clear, toward light color, bland flavor, and soft texture. We have rediscovered in contemporary times the brown and black whole-grain breads of our ancestors, with their chewy textures and assertive flavors, but it is soft white bread that wins the popularity contest, hands down. Europeans may well scoff at the pallid cottony white breads of the commercial American bakery, but it is from Europe that America got her bread traditions. As with so much else, America simply pushed those practices to their inevitable extreme, with bread that is the whitest, the softest, the blandest ever baked. Our "wonder" bread is everything we thought we wanted when we began our long experiment with the cereal grains; Abdoul would surely have been pleased.

If the white bread tradition that began some five thousand years ago in Egypt came to an inevitable conclusion in modern America, the sandwich as a culinary form has a somewhat different history. The invention of our favorite luncheon repast is credited to the fourth Earl of Sandwich, an inveterate gambler who, in his reluctance to leave the gaming table, requested that his meat be brought to him between two slices of bread. The earl's name stuck to the preparation, but the practice is clearly a good deal older than the eighteenth century. Indeed, the French, admittedly not always generous in acknowledging culinary innovation elsewhere, claim credit for the product, if not the name. A recent edition of *Larousse Gastronomique* makes the Gallic pitch:

> Since the most faraway times it has been the custom in the French countryside to give workers in the fields meat for their meal enclosed between two pieces of wholemeal or black bread. Moreover, in all the southwest districts it was customary to provide people setting out on a journey with slices of meat, mostly pork or veal cooked in the pot, enclosed, sprinkled with their succulent juices, between two pieces of bread. Sandwiches made with sardines, tunny fish, anchovies, sliced chicken and even with flat omelettes were known in France well before the word, coming from England, had entered into French culinary terminology.

In medieval England, long before plates and forks were in general use, food was commonly served on trenchers, large square slices of coarse stale bread that were cut from loaves specially baked for the purpose. Diners would help themselves to meat and other foods from bowls on the table, place the food on the trenchers, and eat it with their fingers and sometimes with the aid of knives. The trenchers, thick and stale, absorbed the juice, the grease, and the sauces, and at the end of the meal were either eaten by the diner, thrown to the dogs, or given as alms to the poor. It does not seem a dining experience designed to please the most fastidious, but at least there were no dishes to wash!

The trencher is clearly the forerunner of our open-face sandwich, that classic standby of the roadside diner—piles of tired, warmed-over meat and brown gravy spooned over slices of white bread and meant to be eaten with a knife and fork. Perhaps the earl, in requesting that additional slice of bread to top it all off and make the meal pick-uppable, really does deserve the credit—at least for merrie olde England, where culinary innovation was apparently rare enough to be worthy of comment. But the fundamental idea of the sandwich, the structure of the sandwich—food enclosed by two pieces of bread—is almost certainly a much older one and for very obvious and practical reasons. Sandwiches are portable meals, to be carried on trips where there may be a scarcity of restaurants, kitchens, or cooks, or eaten at work or in the field without the amenities of implements or utensils.

If we look at the wide range of cuisines that produce bread

of some kind, whether leavened or not, we begin to see that the sandwich as a form exists in a large number of varieties and has done so for a long time. Think for a moment of the many ethnic dishes that involve a baked dough of some sort filled or stuffed or wrapped around a filling. Pita pockets stuffed with crisp falafel, chopped vegetables, and sesame sauce. Tortillas wrapped around mashed beans and garnished with fresh chiles and tomatoes. A bagel sliced and spread with cream cheese and lox. A long bun filled with a sausage and garnished with mustard and sauerkraut. Soft steamed Chinese buns stuffed with savory minced roast pork or sweetened bean paste. A hollowed-out loaf of French bread filled with fried oysters and remoulade sauce, a delectable concoction known in New Orleans as a "Po' Boy." All of these dishes are sandwiches, some kind of bread enclosing an almost infinite variety of fillings. We may not ordinarily call a taco or a bagel a sandwich, but a sandwich it is, no different structurally from a BLT on whole wheat toast or a ham and swiss on rye.

Indeed, it is safe to say that wherever there is bread there are sandwiches. The reason has to do with the essential nature of bread, in all its many forms. First, though several breads have characteristic flavors and aromas, they are not ordinarily strong or salient enough to overwhelm the taste and smell of the filling or the enclosed food, which is, after all, the focus, the raison d'être, of the meal; without the meat or the cheese or the savory spread, bread is simply bread. Bread is relatively bland, an appropriately neutral base or housing for the more important filling. Second, bread is absorbent, providing, as it did with the medieval trencher, a convenient catchall for any liquids the food may contain, absorbing those liquids on the inside surface so that each mouthful is juicy and lubricated but with relatively little mess to the diner. Third, and perhaps most critical, bread is dry, providing a whole meal that can be picked up and eaten without the benefit of implements. The smooth, dry, uncontaminated outer surface of the sandwich is the ideal vehicle for a handheld meal; grease, juice, stickiness, and strong food odors are kept where they belong, on the food, not the fingers.

So the sandwich has always functioned as a convenient, easy, quick meal, one that can be consumed on the run, at work or school or on a street corner, with no fuss and little mess—a clear paradigm for "fast" food. But contemporary practice, at least in America, belies the practical origins and traditions of the sandwich, as a convenience meal designed for situations where the customary amenities of dining are not available. For nowadays many of us go to restaurants to eat our sandwiches, sit at tables with plates and silverware and napkins, and order accompanying dishes like cole slaw or potato salad or baked beans that are not particularly portable or pick-uppable. Clearly the sandwich has some appeal that goes beyond its function as a meal on the run, and for that we need no further evidence than almost any sample menu; the sandwich exists in a truly awesome variety, constructed of all manner of breads, buns, and rolls, filled with every conceivable kind of meat, cheese, egg, vegetable, and salad, garnished with an amazing assortment of condiments, spreads, relishes, and sauces. What began no doubt as a simple piece of cold food layered between two slices of bread has burgeoned, in the American experience, into a culinary enterprise that rivals any other for its creative spirit of innovation, and, in the true American fashion, recognizes no cultural or ethnic constraints. Bagel dogs! Chinese tacos! Pita pockets filled with tofu and bean sprouts! My Vietnamese son adorns his bagels with cream cheese, salami, *nuoc mam* (fish sauce), and chile peppers. And if Annie Hall could order a pastrami on white bread with mayo, then as far as the sandwich is concerned, anything goes.

What is it about this particular culinary form that we love so much and that has become so fundamental a part of our daily lives? In addition to the traditional benefits—speed, convenience, portability—why do we find the sandwich so interesting and so appealing? The reasons, I believe, have more to do with aesthetics than with any practical or nutritional concerns. First, the sandwich, even in its simpler forms, offers an exciting adventure in texture and flavor with every mouthful. Layered foods of all kinds tend to provide that, of course, but the sandwich does it particularly well because, more than cooked, sauced, and layered dishes, all the food substances involved remain relatively discrete, retaining their unique flavor and consistency. Think of a chicken club sandwich, for example, with its alternating layers of thin crisp toast, chewy moist chicken salad, crunchy bacon strips, juicy tomato slices, and crisp lettuce. Every bite offers a multitude of textures that would be difficult to obtain with forked or spooned food.

But perhaps most important is that the sandwich offers us the opportunity to be extraordinarily intimate with our food, an opportunity that does not exist with most other foods. Sandwiches are usually grasped with both hands and carried in an upward arc toward the mouth. In this motion it curves directly under the nose, which receives a close, direct waft of the goodies about to be consumed. Unlike food that is eaten with utensils, the sandwich offers a larger amount of food exposed to the nose for a longer period of time, and, once again, the stimulation of our underused nasal organs provides an intense and pleasurable experience, one that heightens the subsequent mouthful with its bounty of flavor and texture. A morsel of food that is speared with a fork, scooped with a spoon, or grasped with chopsticks is brought to the mouth without that close and intimate encounter with the nose and does not provide therefore the same kind of olfactory stimulation. The rules of polite society do not ordinarily encourage us to smell or sniff our food in any obvious fashion (although, interestingly, the appreciation of wine requires the very action that is denied with our food). The sandwich permits us that extra added titillation of the nose and thus offers a richer gustatory experience.

The intimacy of sandwich eating is not merely nasal, of course; the hands, the mouth, and the eyes share as well in this close and compelling involvement with our food. And though many of us may well relish this contact, it is certainly not acceptable in many circumstances and the rules regarding it are at best arbitrary. Will I be thought boorish if I pick up the bone from my porterhouse to gnaw off those last delectable shreds of meat? How is it we can pick up the leaves of the artichoke to dip in the vinaigrette, but we eat the defoliated heart with a knife and fork? How many times have we glanced surreptitiously around the table to see if anyone else is eating those chicken wings with their fingers? We all *want* to do it, but "civilized" behavior denies us that ancient indulgence of tearing into our food with all our parts and senses engaged. Indeed, the only really safe finger food at the table is the bread, which we are required to eat with our hands if we don't want to be thought madly eccentric!

So bread provides, both by itself and as the essential housing for food in the sandwich, a socially sanctioned medium for intimacy with our food that we all seem to covet and to enjoy. And the burger bun accomplishes this with ease. It is a genuine culmination of the bread story, the most refined, enriched, and unobtrusive of baked goods. Its flavor provides a suitably bland base for the savory contents, its texture is soft and pliant yet sturdy enough to stand up to a warm burger with its juicy accompaniments. Its golden brown shape, round and puffed, is a promise of homespun richness, its lack of corners and hard edges an indication of ampleness and generosity, of unconstrained fullness. Yet nothing about the bun gets in the way of the burger itself, no crusty exterior, no yeasty bready aroma, no chewy texture. The bun as bread may not appeal to every taste; indeed, it probably does not appeal to most. But as the crucial support system of the cheeseburger, it fulfills its function admirably—pleasing everyone, offending no one. The burger may be what we're after, that hunk of meat whose juice and grease we atavistically long to coat ourselves with, but it is the bun that mediates between our animal and civilized selves. It is a role most ingeniously conceived.

Three

THE

CHEESE

*T*he eminent English wine and cheese authority T. A. Layton provides in his comprehensive work *The Cheese Handbook* an unusual recipe for cheeseburgers. I quote it in full:

CHEESEBURGERS: This can be one of the finest quick hot meals you have ever had, but you are bound to make a hash of it the first time or so owing to the difficulty of preventing the minced meat from coming apart. But try again; it is worth it and incredibly cheap.

Ingredients: Take, per person, 2 oz. raw mince meat, 1 egg yolk and one segment processed cheese.

The mince meat must be lean and free from stringy bits. Bind the meat with the egg, season with salt and pepper and flatten out to the diameter of a bun and to 1/4 inch thick. You need two of these. Get a slice of cheese to fit the flattened mince meat and smear with mustard. Put the other bit of mince meat on top. Crimp

the edges together and toast under a hot grill both sides.
Serve on a flat dry piece of hot, not buttered, toast.

This has to be—for most Americans, at least—a delightfully
eccentric variation on one of our favorite national dishes,
from the initial cautionary words about the difficulties of dealing with "mince" meat to the final prescription of serving the
burger on a piece of dry toast. Dry toast indeed! But one of
the most interesting elements in this recipe is the cheese—
quite rightly processed cheese—that is sealed within two layers
of the ground meat. The cheese is, in other words, invisible,
and becomes evident to the diner only when the burger is cut
into with a knife and fork. An interesting and not disagreeable
notion, actually, but one that is inimical to the ideal American
cheeseburger, with its golden layer of cheese a deliberate
visual focus, more evident indeed than the meat patty it
blankets.

Curious, isn't it, that while the burger and the bun are
traditionally round, the cheese is most decidedly square? This
is of course no accidental design; the cheese is square so that
when it is placed on the hot beef patty it melts ever so slightly
and the four points of the square droop invitingly off the
round edge of the burger. Those four small golden triangles
are all that we see, but they are enough to point to yet another
layer of gustatory richness, different from the burger yet
somehow complementary to it. It is an unlikely and unex-

pected addition, but it has an important role to play in this tangible reconstruction of our culinary history.

Cheese is peculiar stuff, and for a couple of very good reasons. The material from which it is made and the way it is made are unique; both the substance and the process are unavailable and indeed inconceivable as adult food to any creature except the aberrant human, with his inclination and ability to fashion good eats out of any number of unlikely materials. Cheese, like bread, is one of those exquisite creations of human culture; unlike bread, however, it is far less universally appealing and for the most part a good deal more complicated to make.

Milk is the stuff from which cheese is made, and milk is a substance produced by mammalian mothers as a food for newborn infants and dependent young. In nature's design milk has no other function and no further potential; it occurs in the mother as a result of hormonal changes during pregnancy and birth and is produced in direct response to the suckling of nursing infants. When the young become capable of eating normal adult food, they are more or less gradually weaned from the teat, and the production of milk dries up, to recur only with another pregnancy and another birth. It is an effective and efficient system—nourishing, easily consumed food produced directly by the mother for an amount of time necessary for the infant to become a self-sufficient feeder. Other animals—birds, for example—also feed their young, but they must fly off to hunt for the food, then predigest it and ultimately regurgitate the mash to feed the chicks. It is a laborious and time-consuming enterprise compared to the mammalian system of lactation.

Once weaned from the teat or the udder, the young mammal never again has access to milk, which remains exclusively a food for nursing infants. Only humans altered nature's design and did so, it would seem, fairly early in their history. It is not difficult to imagine how it might have occurred, as the behavior of lactating mammals is not very different from that of lactating human females; the suckling of infants is much the same, no matter what the species. Indeed, it is entirely possible that the initial exchange was quite the opposite of what we might expect; anthropologists indicate that lactating human mothers suckled orphaned animals like piglets and wolf cubs, who were then raised as members of the household. Since dogs were domesticated before most meat and dairy animals, it is not unlikely that newborn pups who had lost their own mother might have been suckled by human mothers; it happens even to this day in traditional cultures like those of New Guinea.

At any rate, we know that most of our common dairy animals were domesticated beginning about ten thousand years ago, starting, probably, with sheep and goats, then extending to cows, horses, water buffalo, yak, camels, and reindeer. Once there was a breeding population of animals in close contact with humans, the advantages of excess milk from a lactating mammal would have been obvious. If a human mother died in childbirth and there were no other lactating females to suckle the newborn infant, it would die unless it was somehow supplied with adequate nourishment. This could be accomplished by softening or processing adult food into a paste that was then placed on the infant's tongue, or by providing a naturally soft, smooth, digestible substance. The Byzantine historian Procopius, for example, reported on a tribe of "savage" Lapps who routinely fed their newborns not with milk but with bone marrow. But milk is the ideal and the easiest food for suckling infants and many motherless newborns must have been saved by the milk from the family's herds.

The exchange between humans and their lactating animals doubtless went two ways. Many herd animals typically produce more milk than they need, and if a newborn calf were to sicken or die, the mother would be left with the pain and discomfort of bloated, distended udders. Milking by human hands would provide relief and at the same time, of course, prolong lactation. The more you milk, the more milk you get, and it would surely not have taken very long for people to realize that they had to consume or store the excess milk; it seems unlikely that our ancestors would have spilled or wasted so valuable and so potent a substance. Milk has been called, after all, the ideal or perfect food because, with only minimal supplements like iron and some vitamins, it provides generous amounts of the nutrients necessary for humans to grow and prosper—high-quality protein, carbohydrate, and fat, as well as calcium, phosphorus, and vitamin A. And if milk was so good for human infants, then why not for human adults?

The answer, as we must have rather quickly discovered, is that nature did not design milk as a food for adults, and, as we are still learning, it's not a good idea to fool with Mother Nature. The problem is that all the carbohydrate in milk is in the form of a sugar called lactose. To break down that sugar and render it digestible, an enzyme called lactase is required. If the sugar is not broken down by the enzyme, it can cause severe cramps, diarrhea, and gastric distension. Under these circumstances milk, if consumed in substantial amounts, can be not only useless nutritionally but actually detrimental; the rapid emptying of the gut results not only in the loss of the milk as nourishment but also in the loss of nutrients from other foods that have not yet been completely absorbed.

All infants, human and animal, produce the lactase enzyme in their bodies and so are able to digest the milk that is their first and frequently only food. But after weaning, the body's production of the enzyme diminishes, and at various ages from about five years or so on may cease almost entirely. From the body's point of view decreased production of the enzyme makes perfectly good sense; why continue to produce something you no longer have any need for? After all, both human and animal children must eventually learn to eat ordinary adult food, and the discomfort caused by partially undigested milk may well be the body's way to encourage weaning. At any rate, when lactase production drops off, the human system is no longer capable of digesting milk satisfactorily, and if substantial amounts are consumed, severe gastric discomfort may result. The same is true for other mammals, which is why your veterinarian advises you not to feed milk to your adult cats and dogs.

This condition is known as lactose malabsorption, and although originally it was probably almost universal, it is by no means so in human populations today. We all know adults who can consume large quantities of milk without so much as a twinge, a sure indication that their bodies are still producing lactase. In fact, there are whole groups of people, primarily of Western and Northern European extraction, who consume milk without any apparent ill effects. The ability to produce the lactase enzyme into adulthood appears to have a racial basis and to be genetically determined; some groups have it and some don't, and the trait is passed from generation to generation.

The interesting thing is that there seems to be a clear correlation between people who retain the enzyme into adulthood and people who have a long history of dairying—that is, who domesticated certain herd animals for the purpose of using their milk as food. For example, most African blacks are lactose intolerant, unable as adults to digest fresh milk satisfactorily. Yet the Masai and other traditional pastoral herdsmen who have long sustained themselves on the blood and milk of their cattle, are lactose tolerant, a clearly adaptive trait for people who live largely on milk. It is thought that over many long generations those individuals who milked domesticated animals and were lactose tolerant were more likely to survive and propagate than those who were lactose intolerant, and that gradually the trait for lactose tolerance became dominant in the group. At any rate, the development of the trait is linked to the practice of dairying and is largely absent in people who never developed a strong tradition of dairying—much of the population of Southeast Asia, Africa, and, of course, aboriginal America, where dairy animals were completely unknown until they were introduced by the Spanish after 1492.

Despite this clear correlation, there are groups of people who, like the Greeks, for example, have a long history of herding and dairying and yet remain, to this day, largely lactose intolerant. The question is why this should be so, and the answers have largely to do with the crucial processes by which people transformed milk into other more acceptable substances. Remember that lactose malabsorption develops in response to fresh milk because of the body's inability to break down the milk sugars. And it must be noted that there are large and striking individual differences in sensitivity; some people experience only mild discomfort while others cannot tolerate even small amounts. But what if the lactose could be broken down into more digestible compounds by means other than an enzyme that may or may not be present in our digestive systems? Then we might have access to all the nutritive value of milk, with its rich storehouse of protein, fat, and carbohydrate, without so many of the ill effects that the lack of the lactase enzyme produces. If we break down the lactose before we eat the milk, then we don't need the enzyme and we have made available to ourselves a grand new source of wonderful nourishing food, as valuable as the meat from the animals that produce it.

And this is exactly the way it seems to have happened in history, again one of those accidental but somehow inevitable discoveries that made the human food experience so elaborate and so unique. The scene is traditionally set in the Near East, not unreasonably, as this was the area of the world in which the primary dairy animals—sheep, goats, and cattle—were first domesticated. The discovery is attributed to an anonymous Arab who, having stashed a supply of milk in an intestinal paunch that he attached to his saddle, rode off across the hot desert sands. At the end of the day when he went to drink his milk he was not a little surprised to find that his liquid meal had changed to a semi-solid mass with a creamy soft texture and an agreeably tart but mild flavor. Infant food grown up! What started out as fresh sweet milk turned into some form of yogurt or fresh cheese; not only was it solid food rather than liquid but much of the lactose had been broken down into simpler, more digestible sugars.

We don't know for sure when the culturing of milk began, but it would certainly not have been long after the domestication of milk-producing animals. Milk is very perishable, particularly in warm climates, and the extraordinary advantages of cultured milk products would have quickly become obvious. They can be stored for longer periods without spoilage, they are more compact and are thus easier to transport, and they offer an extremely valuable and concentrated source of nourishment. And the problem of lactose malabsorption, for many people who could not digest fresh milk, was easily and effectively solved. What happened to that nameless ancient's milk was a twofold process that would lead eventually to the golden slice on, or in, our favorite burger.

We know that our ancestors used intestinal paunches as watertight storage containers; these sacs, particularly the multiple stomach paunches of herbivorous animals, contain rennin, an enzyme that is capable of coagulating milk proteins when the milk is appropriately acidic. The bacteria that are normally found in milk will produce lactic acid in warm temperatures; the churning action of a galloping horse would no doubt have speeded up the process. Once the milk became acidic, the rennin went to work coagulating the milk solids or curds and separating them from the liquid or whey. The whey, which contains little of the nutritive value of the milk, would be poured off and the remaining solids eaten as a form of fresh cheese, or used as the starting material for a cured or ripened cheese.

Except for such fresh cheeses as cottage cheese, cream cheese, farmer's cheese, ricotta, and so forth, most of the cheeses with which we are familiar are cured and fall into four basic categories: soft (Brie, Camembert), semisoft (Muenster, Port du Salut, Roquefort), hard (Swiss, cheddar), and very hard or grating (Parmesan, Romano). All cured cheeses are made in basically the same way. The coagulated milk curds are pressed and salted, then ripened by different kinds of bacteria, mold, or surface microorganisms under controlled conditions of heat and humidity for varying amounts of time. The characteristic blue or green veins in Gorgonzola and Roquefort, for example, are caused by kinds of mold introduced into the pressed milk curds, while the holes in Emmentaler or Gruyère are caused by bacteria that ripen the cheese and give it its unique flavor and texture. There are of course hundreds of different kinds of cheese. Each owes its unique characteristics of flavor, aroma, texture, and color to a number of variables, such as the type of milk-producing animal and the pasturage on which it feeds, the butterfat content of the milk, the amount of salt and acidity, the type of microorganism used for curing, and the duration of the ripening process. The range of sensory attributes of cheese is enormous, from creamy to crumbly, bland to tart, subtle to smelly, and because of the wide variety of gustatory experiences it affords, cheese is used in many ways—as a basic food, as a seasoning ingredient, and as a savory garnish or enrichment for other foods. So fundamental did it become in France as the appropriate finale to a meal that the eighteenth-century gastronome Brillat-Savarin declared: "Dessert without cheese is like a pretty girl with only one eye."

Cheese, along with its attendant cultured milk products like yogurt and sour cream, became entrenched as a highly desirable food in specific cultures and areas of the world where the domestication of dairy animals was a practical and useful enterprise—most of Europe, the Near and Middle East, Central Asia, and of course ultimately America. It is interesting that while the culturing of milk effectively solved the problem of lactose malabsorption for a great many people, there were also those in different parts of the world who never accepted cheese as a viable food, even though it is clearly a valuable nutritional alternative to animal flesh and fat. The reasons for the failure of cheese to find acceptance in many of these groups may have less to do with physiology than with a cultural rejection of food that was unfamiliar and thought to be distasteful. The Mongols, those fierce horsemen of the Asian steppes, lived largely on cultured milk products—yogurt, curds, cheese, and a fermented alcoholic beverage made from mare's milk and called koumiss—but these foods never really took hold in mainstream China, even though the Mongols overran and occupied China for several hundred years. The Chinese regarded cultured milk products as barbarian food, as from their point of view it surely was. To this day it is common for chauvinistic Westerners to refer to tofu, which is soybean curd and is a valuable Chinese staple food that is nonfermented, as "equivalent" to cheese, presumably because it is light in color and high in protein. But cheese and tofu are very dissimilar foods from the sensory, the culinary, and the gastronomic points of view; just imagine stir-frying a cube of Velveeta or garnishing a bowl of onion soup with shredded bean curd!

More significant, perhaps, than the fact that milk products were unfamiliar to nondairying cultures is that cheese belongs to a group of highly manipulated man-made foods that uses spoilage or rotting as a technique of production. Most cuisines have some foods that are produced by the controlled action of various microorganisms. Beer, wine, and vinegar are the most obvious and widespread examples, as is the leavened bread produced by the fermentive action of yeast. Soy sauce and soy paste (miso), those seasoning compounds found in so much of Chinese and Japanese cooking, are made from soybeans and a variety of grains, salted, fermented, and aged. Tempeh is a fermented soybean cake widely used in Indonesian cookery.

Animal as well as plant substances can be effectively ripened with microorganisms. The Eskimos traditionally fermented some of their ocean harvest; a morsel of "high" seal blubber was considered a great delicacy, one offered to honored guests. More familiar to us are the fish sauces of Southeast Asia, Vietnamese *nuoc mam* and Thai *nam pla,* made from salted fermented fish, usually anchovies, that are aged and strained and used as an indispensable seasoning agent. Similarly, the cuisine of ancient Rome depended heavily on fermented fish sauces known as *garum* or *liquamen,* which were used to season both sweet and savory dishes. And the fabled "thousand-year-old" eggs of the Chinese are uncooked eggs that are buried in ash, lime, and horse-piss-soaked straw for several months; when the eggs are shelled, they are dark, pungent, and "cheesy" in flavor and aroma.

The adjective *cheesy* is a significant one that we use to imply that something about the product (or the unwashed body) is "off" or spoiled, and that is a characteristic shared by most fermented or ripened foods, particularly those of animal origin. What seems ripe (or good) to me may seem rotten (or bad) to you, and that issue of taste or sensibility is largely culturally constrained. Many Asians regard thousand-year-old eggs as a toothsome delicacy, while disdaining cheese as nothing more than rotten milk. Similarly, the average Frenchman may delight in any number of smelly, runny cheeses but would probably not be too enthralled with a mouthful of putrid seal meat crawling with maggots. It's all a matter of taste, of tradition, of individual and cultural preference, and the fact is that cheese, like many other fermented animal substances, is not by any means a universally accepted food.

If that is the case, then how did a slice of cheese get to be a part of the cheeseburger composition, that collection of foods that seems to have such widespread appeal, even to cultures that do not generally regard cheese as a desirable substance? The answer is that the cheeseburger's cheese is about as uncheesy as it is possible to be and still be called cheese—and there's a mouthful! But we still have a way to go before we get to our beloved burger's golden slice.

America has become one of the largest cheese producers in the world, manufacturing an enormous variety of cheese, both fresh and cured. Although there have been a number of genuine innovations by American cheesemakers, most of the cheeses are modeled on European varieties, primarily from France, Italy, Switzerland, Holland, Germany, and Scandinavia—the great dairying regions of Europe. But America's strongest cheese traditions come, not surprisingly, from England, which gave us our early colonists and our first mainstream culture. The English have been for centuries great consumers of cheese, which surely functioned along with other dairy products as a useful and savory alternative to meat. The residents of the British Isles have a special fondness for toasted and melted cheese dishes that have become a familiar part of the American tradition—grilled cheese sandwiches, macaroni and cheese, and that old classic, Welsh rarebit, so named because a nobleman who ran out of game to serve his guests substituted melted cheese on toast and called it "Welsh rabbit." There is good reason for the great popularity of melted cheese; although it is no different nutritionally from the unmelted, it offers a distinctly different sensory experience. The semiliquefaction of the fat portion of the cheese provides a rich, smooth, sensual texture, an unctuous mouth feel that is extremely appealing.

Until this century most English cheeses were produced in individual farms or small town cooperatives, and of the many varieties made it was the cheddar or cheddar types (Cheshire, Darby, Welsh Caerphilly) for which England is most famous and which became the model for the most popular American cheeses. In this country cheeses of this category were called not only cheddar, but brick, colby, longhorn, coon, or rat cheese, and, when sold in stores, as store cheese. Excellent varieties of the type are produced in Vermont, New York, Wisconsin, and Canada. Eventually some of the cheeses became known as American cheddar, and from that name it was but a small step to American cheese. American cheese was

no doubt once a recognizable descendant of its parent cheddar, but it has come in recent times to signify a unique product of the American food industry that many cheese
connoisseurs would disclaim as belonging to the great family
of "real" cheeses, a product that the American critic Clifton
Fadiman once called "solidified floor wax."

This is "processed" cheese or processed cheese food, a
uniquely American development, sold in rectangular one- or
two-pound loaves, or packaged in unerringly square slices
between sealed sheets of plastic wrap. Processed cheese is
made by grinding up different kinds of cheese, usually Swiss
and cheddar types, then pasteurizing the resulting mixture to
prevent any further microbial action. Gums, emulsifiers, and
stabilizers may be added, as well as milk solids or cream that
enrich the cheese. The result is a cheese food that is bland
and smooth, with a uniform flavor and texture, good melting
qualities, and a long shelf life. It was originally designed in
the early years of the century by James L. Kraft, a Chicago
cheese merchant, as a "scientific" approach to the mass marketing of cheese; and as the company he founded has become
the world's largest cheese manufacturer, his idea must be
acknowledged as a commercial, if not gastronomic, success.
Processed cheese has been extraordinarily popular, in part
because of its appeal to children; although it lacks the highly
aromatic and flavorful qualities of traditional cheeses, its
smooth, mild character makes it easily acceptable to finicky

young palates. And until only recently cheese in America was thought to be an ideal food for growing children because, as a concentrated form of milk, it provides all the nutritional benefits of milk in a palatable easy-to-eat solid form.

It is a little curious, then, that while cheese is conceptualized in America as concentrated milk, its preferred color, at least in the processed form, is very different from the color of milk. Milk is white, sometimes almost bluish white, while the most popular cheese slices are a deep golden orange hue. Is this some fanciful marketing strategy, a gimmick designed by the food industry to titillate the palate by intriguing the eye, like multicolored pasta or blue cupcake frosting or clear cola drinks? Or is the bright color a flag for youthful consumers, whose sometimes aberrant preferences condition so many aspects of American culture? Actually, while all these possibilities may be involved, the coloring of cheese is not an invention to which America can lay claim; it is a tradition we inherited from our English forebears.

While all cheese is made from milk, one of the critical variables is the butterfat content, which can vary significantly in both quantity and quality from animal to animal, from breed to breed, from region to region, and from season to season. Butterfat generally ranges in color from a creamy white to a pale yellow to light gold; the variations in color have to do with greater or lesser amounts of carotenes in the fat. Carotenes are yellow- or orange-pigmented chemicals that are precursors of vitamin A and are most concentrated in carrots, sweet potatoes, red and yellow peppers, and some kinds of winter squash, as well as in a variety of dark green vegetables such as broccoli, spinach, collards, and kale. Because the carotenes are fat soluble, their most abundant source in animal foods are egg yolks and cream; dairy animals that have fed on fresh green summer pasturage produce cream that is richer in carotenes, and hence more deeply pigmented, than the cream from animals that have fed on dry winter fodder.

The early farm producers of cheddar cheese in England understood the relationship between pasturage and the color of the butterfat; in the seventeenth century a particularly fine cheddar type called "morning" cheese was produced from the milk of summer-fed cows with the addition of extra butterfat, a source of even more carotene. The cheese was deeply colored and exceptionally rich. Other cheesemakers attempted to emulate this richness by less expensive means: They colored their cheese artificially with extracts from carrots and nasturtiums, and later with annatto, the tiny red seeds of a tropical American tree. Called *achiote* in Mexican and Caribbean cuisine, annatto was an indigenous New World product that is still used by Native Americans to color their food; the seeds release their deep golden color when heated in oil, a technique common to much West Indian cookery, or they can be ground up with other ingredients to make *adobos,* red seasoning pastes used widely in Mexican cuisine. When annatto was introduced into Europe, it was used, as it still is today, to impart a more deeply yellow or orange pigment to cheese, to deceive the buyer, as one eighteenth-century English critic complained, into thinking that the cheese "contained more richness" than it actually did.

The tradition of producing cheddars of both the natural pale creamy color and the artificially colored yellow-orange was transported to America, where it was incorporated into the manufacture of American cheese and processed cheese. There is no nutritive difference between the two, but the more deeply colored variety may be an ancient trigger for what is perceived as added value, richness, and better quality. (It is worth noting that yellow and gold have long been highly valued as food colors. Indian and Malaysian cuisine rely heavily on turmeric as a yellow coloring agent, and many cultures use saffron, the most expensive spice in the world, to provide a rich golden hue. Medieval European cooks delighted in golden or "endored" preparations; they gilded festive foods with pastes made of egg yolks and saffron.) An executive at the Kraft Cheese Company informs me that the orange cheese is by far the most popular throughout the country, save only for the Northeast, which eccentrically prefers the white. And it is of course the more deeply colored variety that is the cheese of choice on the cheeseburger.

Just as the color of the cheese is a signal for something

more, something better, something richer, the cheese itself is an added bonus, an extravagant additional layer that is there to provide sensory gratification and not because it is necessary. Cheese, like meat, is a savory and efficient package of high-quality protein and fat, but from the long perspective on human history, meat and cheese are to a large extent mutually exclusive foods. Except, perhaps, for the aristocracy or the privileged elite, most ordinary people in traditional cultures would surely not have had the means to enjoy two such valuable foods in the same meal, much less in the same dish. And history shows that where dairy products were produced, cheese was used as a viable and satisfactory substitute for meat, not as a companion food. Indeed, some cuisines have ritualized the separation of the two kinds of food: Traditional pastoral cultures like the Masai of East Africa and the ancient Jews of the Near East forbid the consumption of dairy products, which are made from the living food of living animals, in conjunction with meat, which is the dead flesh of dead animals. Whatever the reasons—ritual, social, economic—for not eating meat and cheese together, they may reflect a deeper understanding that the combination of these two power-packed foods is a kind of nutritional overkill, unnecessary, unaffordable, and in some profound way, unseemly.

And that may be, in the end, exactly why we put a slice of cheese on the burger, as gustatory proof that nothing is denied. Even though cheese is not everyone's choice of good food, even though it is by no stretch of the imagination a universally appealing substance, even though *this* cheese contains more lactose in the form of added milk solids than other cheeses, it has insinuated itself into the gastronomic experience of many who one might think would reject it. It has accomplished this by being sanitized, or decheesified, as it were. It has severely diminished or eliminated those salient sensory attributes of flavor and aroma that may be offensive to noncheese eaters, while retaining the characteristics that make it more widely attractive—its golden color and its smooth, unctuous melting fatty texture. The cheese is not there for its valuable protein content but for yet another gustatory sensation of fat, an added dimension of the sensual eating pleasure we humans have always craved.

The cheese is a clear affirmation of the total indulgence that the cheeseburger as a whole represents, and the golden triangles are signposts of excess, pointing to a gustatory experience of overabundance.

Four

THE

KETCHUP

Although we may rightly perceive the cheeseburger, with all its parts, as thoroughly American, it may come as a surprise to discover that at least one of its major components has distinctly exotic origins, with roots in more distant and foreign cultures and traditions than the beef and cheese of Europe and the leavened white bread of the Near East. And it is ironic indeed that this more exotic component is the one most commonly associated with America and American food—our beloved all-purpose condiment, ketchup. The slender soldierly bottle with its jaunty white cap, flaunting its rich crimson contents, is known and recognized all over the world, valued for what it is and what it represents, the proud scarlet standard of the American experience.

But before we investigate how ketchup got to be ketchup, and the reasons for its emergence as both the substance and the symbol of twentieth-century America, we need to look at a whole category of foods to which it belongs and an ancient tradition of culinary practice from which it was born, for both are unique and unprecedented in the animal kingdom. Ketchup, along with its large extended family of condiments, sauces, spices, and seasonings, has little to do with nourishment per se, but involves rather the pervasive practice of enhancing or altering or intensifying the *flavor* of food. The components of the cheeseburger that we have looked at so far—the meat, the cheese, the bread—are all, no matter the vicissitudes of their origin and evolution, basic foods, foods that we use to nourish ourselves. But the ketchup is quite another story. It is not there to fill our bellies or satisfy our hunger, but to tickle our tongues and please our palates, to make the rest of the food taste better.

We don't really know how or why people first began to flavor their food deliberately by adding other substances. The most widely used and pervasive seasoning ingredient is, of course, salt, and it may have been the first that humans sought in their quest for more palatable sustenance. The taste for salt is one we share with other mammals, and it may be that our bodies' specific requirement for sodium conditioned our initial positive response to it. Still, it is clear from past evidence and contemporary practice that our consumption of salt is far greater than nutritional needs dictate, and that added salt provides gratification of quite another kind, that of flavor enhancement. Quite simply, salt makes food taste better—to the human consumer, at least—and has always done so. It not only adds its own saltiness, but it also blocks some bitter tastes and may reveal or enhance other more desirable flavors. Whether our first exposure to salt came from seawater or from dried mineral deposits we will never know, but it has always been the most central and the most universal of seasonings, so valued that it was sometimes used as a form of currency: Our word *salary* comes from the Latin word for "salt," used to pay the wages of Roman soldiers.

In addition to salt there are hundreds of substances that have been used to alter or enhance the flavor of food, apparently from the earliest periods of our history. In our relentless search for new and valuable sources of nourishment, we stumbled on all manner of roots and leaves, berries and fruits, barks and seeds, that had attractive aromas and flavors and that we may have employed initially for other purposes. These many plant substances served, as they still do today, as fumigants, perfumes, or air fresheners, or were burned as fragrant offerings to the gods. Many herbs and spices were used in ancient Egypt as part of the embalming process, and vanilla beans, the dried fermented pods of a tropical orchid native to the New World, were sometimes hung in pre-Columbian Mexican homes to scent the air with their sweet aroma. Many herbs and spices served ritual or medicinal purposes, and these substances are still highly regarded by many cultures for their special beneficial or curative powers. Cloves still sweeten the breath, as they have done for many thousands of years, and chile peppers are still considered to be an effective aphrodisiac by some Native American people. Garlic has long been thought to be a potent antiflatulent agent in India, while in modern America it is valued by many as an effective anticholesterant and sold in deodorized nonculinary tablet form.

Whatever their initial use or significance, many of these substances gradually became appreciated for their positive effects on food (or on the palate), and however their flavoring properties were first discovered, their use as seasonings is clearly an ancient one. From studies of fossilized plant remains, for example, comes evidence that the native people of Mexico have been spicing their food (as well as their sex lives) with chile peppers for many thousands of years, and sophisticated paleobotanical studies have begun to show how the pungent little fruits of an indigenous wild plant were gradually domesticated for use as a seasoning agent. In China, where unfortunately the scientific record is not so complete, the rhizome of the ginger plant seems to have flavored food for a time well before written history records its use as a common kitchen herb. Fossilized remains of caraway and poppy seeds have been found in prehistoric dwellings in Switzerland, and a rich trove of spices, herbs, and aromatics has been cultivated in India, Malaysia, and the Spice Islands for as long as the archaeological record extends; there is evidence that the seasoning ingredients for Indian curries have been exported to other parts of the world for several thousand years.

What is amazing about this record is not only the longevity of the seasoning enterprise among humankind, but the consistency of the practice in individual traditions. Chile peppers are still the most widely used seasoning ingredient in Mexico. Gingerroot is pervasive in all of Chinese and much derivative Oriental cuisine. Poppy and caraway seeds are still widely used in Central European cookery. And the spices and aromatics most commonly found in Indian curries are much the same today as they were those many centuries ago; the flavor and aroma of cumin, coriander, turmeric, ginger, garlic, and cloves are as appealing today as they apparently were in ancient times. What we have here is clear testimony that people not only care deeply about flavoring their food but also that once they have achieved or obtained a satisfactory way of doing it, they stick with it, embracing certain flavors with tenacity and avoiding others with equal fervor. It would be as unlikely for a Chinese person to season his noodles with sour cream and dill as it would be for a Swede to flavor his herring with soy sauce and gingerroot. Food habits and preferences do change, of course, but traditional flavoring practices tend to be conservative and carefully maintained.

When we look at seasoning practices from the broad perspective, what we see is a frequent use of certain characteristic combinations of flavoring ingredients in different ethnic traditions. Chinese cooking, for example, has long employed the combination of soy sauce, rice wine, and gingerroot as a basic and central seasoning compound, one that is evident throughout the many regions and cooking styles of China. The basic theme is frequently varied with the use of other ingredients—garlic, vinegar, sugar, sesame, hoisin—but the underlying flavor theme remains constant. Another set of seasoning compounds occurs in the Mediterranean, where the intimate bond of olive oil and tomatoes is varied from cuisine to cuisine with a variety of other flavors—garlic, basil, and oregano in southern Italy, lemon and cinnamon in Greece, rosemary, sage, and thyme in southern France.

Indeed, these characteristic combinations of flavoring ingredients, which I call Flavor Principles, can be seen in almost any cuisine we choose to look at: onions, lard, and paprika in Hungarian cooking; fish sauce, lemon, and chile in Vietnamese cooking; peanuts, peppers, and tomatoes in West African food; soy sauce, coconut, and curry spices in Malaysian cuisines. The same seasonings are combined over and over again so consistently in a given cuisine that they begin to function as a kind of sensory label for prepared food, a way of providing identity and familiarity. And all people, no matter who they are or where they come from, seem to find it important to provide their food with a good and proper taste, one that is consistent and familiar. (The philosopher Wittgenstein is reported to have said, "I don't care what I eat as long as it always tastes the same.")

For both the educated and the naive taster, there can be

little doubt that the flavors of soy sauce and sesame oil are very different from those of tomato sauce and Parmesan cheese, and that both are clearly distinguishable from yogurt and mint or lamb fat and cinnamon. The details of the seasoning enterprise are widely divergent and have their origins in geography, climate, food resources, and cooking traditions, established and maintained over many generations. But even in the face of the staggering variety of seasoning ingredients and the details of individual ethnic traditions, we cannot help being struck by the universality of the practice. Everybody does it, in one way or another, consistently altering, modifying, transforming, enhancing the flavor of food. Why? What is it about being human that makes flavor, with all its complexity, so interesting and so meaningful?

There is some good reason to understand seasoning as a uniquely human response to "imperfect" food. All people, all cultures, have beliefs about what the best food is: the purest virgin oil, the firstborn lamb of the flock, the tenderest baby vegetables pearled with morning dew. The "best" can be defined in many ways, as the youngest or the rarest or the purest or the costliest or the most nutritionally valuable, and it has always been reserved for the gods in ritual offerings, for the powerful and privileged of the culture, or presented, like the sheep eyes in traditional Arab cuisine, to honored guests as an expression of hospitality.

No matter how the best and the finest may be defined by

any cultural tradition, the fact is that most ordinary people do not usually have access to it, and it is seasoning that frequently functions as a way of making less-than-perfect food more acceptable and more satisfying. The Chinese, for many centuries the widely acknowledged masters of the culinary arts, categorize flavor in two basic ways. The first, and best, is the flavor inherent in the finest of food substances—the highest quality fresh meat, the choicest animal bones, the most delicate new vegetables—flavor that is coaxed and nurtured with consummate skill, care, time, and expense. This kind of food and this kind of flavor—subtle, complex, "natural," refined—is very different from the other kind, which is called "cheap" flavor. It relies not on the finest ingredients or the most skillful technique, but on strong, salient seasoning substances that are quickly and easily fashioned into savory, mouth-filling sauces and condiments that turn imperfect or unsatisfying foods into palatable and pleasurable eating experiences.

And it is of course "cheap" flavor that most of the world, of necessity, enjoys. It is familiar kitchen practice no matter where we come from—stewing scanty, cheap, tough cuts of meat in highly seasoned savory sauces, making piquant condiments or relishes out of bruised or leftover fruits and vegetables, then using those condiments to enhance other foods, perking up a pot of boiled beans or grains or starchy tubers with zesty salsas or just a sprinkle of hot chile peppers. Whatever the food and whatever the cultural beliefs that tell us how to make it better, the addition or enhancement of flavor seems to be primary in its capacity to make food taste "right."

When we look at the broad spectrum of human flavoring practices, we see one very curious correlation: The heavier the dependence on plant or vegetable foods, the more pronounced the seasonings; the heavier the consumption of animal foods, the less pronounced the seasonings. Those cuisines that clearly demonstrate a highly spiced or complex seasoning profile—Southeast Asia, India, Africa, Mexico—all have long relied on high-plant, low-meat diets. Conversely, the heavy meat and dairy food cultures of Northern and Western Europe and of Central Asia show less salient, more underplayed flavoring practices. It looks as though the heavier seasoning of vegetable foods is a way of compensating for the lack of animal food, and more specifically, of red meat. This compensation is not nutritional, however; it is gustatory.

The correlation is reinforced when we look at one of the greatest "cheap" seasonings the world has ever known, the chile peppers. Native to Mexico, Central America, and South America, the pungent capsicums had been used for many thousands of years by the indigenous people of the New World to perk up their basic diet of corn, cassava, beans, and squashes. The peppers were hybridized into dozens of varieties, each with its own unique flavor and hotness, the pungency provided by a chemical called capsaicin that is found in the inner membranes of the pepper and, to a lesser extent, in the seeds and the flesh. The chiles are eaten fresh, pickled, roasted, dried, and smoked, and are used as a simple condiment or added to salsas, soups, and stews. These extraordinary seasoning ingredients not only offer a wide range of flavors but also have the capacity to stimulate or irritate the mucous membranes of the tongue, the palate, the lips, and the throat; it is this irritant characteristic that seems to up the ante on the flavor experience. The chiles reached their fullest level of development in the regional cuisines of Mexico, which continue today as they have for untold generations to exploit the complexity of the peppers' flavor and pungency.

But chile peppers, so widely and intensely used in the Americas, were unknown outside the New World before Columbus's landing in the Bahamas in 1492. They were brought back to Spain and from there made their way around the world, carried from port to port by Spanish and Portuguese navigators. Within thirty to fifty years of their discovery in the Americas, chile peppers had become firmly established in many of the cultures and cuisines of the world that were already cultivating heavy seasoning as a response to high-vegetable, low-meat diets—India, Africa, Southeast Asia. The pattern of acceptance, the level of enthusiasm with which the pungent chiles were enfolded into certain existing traditions, seems to indicate that the unique stimulation they provide is an important compensation for foods that are somehow less satisfying, less perfect, when eaten unseasoned. And on the other hand, the chiles were largely ignored or rejected by cuisines and areas of the world where meat and other animal foods were a significant focus of the diet.

If this account of the chile pepper, with its intriguing patterns of acceptance and rejection throughout the world after 1492, seems to lend support to the notion that strong seasoning traditions correlate with low meat and animal food diets, it corroborates as well our response to the burger itself. For we began our investigation of the cheeseburger platter with the argument that red meat, bathed with fat and bloody juices, is of compelling universal interest, representing a kind of perfection in the human food experience. And though that ideal may have its roots in biological or nutritional concerns, it obviously became hooked into the sensory and aesthetic dimensions of our eating behavior. If juicy red meat was what we craved but couldn't always get, we found or devised elaborate and sophisticated substitutes that provided equivalent kinds of sensory and aesthetic gratification. These had largely to do with heightened flavor, with intensified seasoning practices, whose appeal was not only gustatory but also strongly visual.

When we look at cuisines that have traditionally depended more heavily on plant rather than animal foods, we find not only higher seasoning but high color—red, reddish brown,

brown, golden brown—the very colors characteristic of meat. Think once again of those cuisines we have already described as fundamentally vegetable based and imagine the visual attributes of the sauces and condiments that are so basic a part of the cooking traditions: the red chile, tomato, and *achiote* sauces of Mexico; the rich brown soy sauces and pastes of the Orient; the ruddy tomato sauces of the Mediterranean and the Middle East; the colorful gold and orange curries of India and Malaysia. If people are forced by economic, geographic, or ritual constraints to live largely on rice or beans or corn or cassava, they do so more happily if those plant foods, with their bland flavors and starchy or mealy textures, are beefed up (*now* the expression is perfectly clear) with extra flavor for the mouth *and* added color for the eye.

It is interesting, then, that along with the chile pepper, an unparalleled super stimulus for the palate, the New World was also the ancestral home of a food that was a super stimulus for the eye. That food was, of course, the tomato, red and juicy, an unprecedented vegetable source of visual as well as gustatory appeal. Cooked into a variety of sauces, it provides a flavor that is round and full, slightly salty and mildly acidic, and an appearance that is rich and meaty, ruddy and intense. In the early decades of the twentieth century, when the tomato became widely hybridized in America, many varieties were designated as "beefsteak" because of their similarity to a juicy slab of beef. Indeed, no other plant product is so profoundly meatlike in certain crucial attributes, which may well explain the tomato's capacity to evoke both tremendous enthusiasm and deep antipathy.

Introduced to Europe after the discovery and conquest of Mexico in 1519 by Hernán Cortés and his conquistadores, the tomato elicited a fascinating variety of responses. In Southern Europe and the entire region of the Mediterranean it seems to have been accepted in fairly short order, grown as a common garden crop and enthusiastically incorporated into already existing seasoning traditions. This is an area where olive oil was and still is king, where the robust flavors of garlic and onion, a variety of herbs and spices, nuts and citrus fruits, complemented a diet based on grains in the form of bread, pasta, rice, and porridges made of whole grains and legumes. The tomato, treated as a vegetable by these Mediterranean cuisines, was cooked into a variety of richly flavored savory sauces that clearly enhanced a diet that was not lacking in flavor but was deficient in color and visual appeal.

In the rest of Europe the story was very different. The tomato was largely rejected, and even thought to be poisonous because it is a member of a family of plants that includes the deadly nightshade. But those areas of Europe that rejected the tomato are the very same areas that accepted the potato, another New World export that was introduced at the same time and is also a member of the nightshade family. So the poisonous nightshade connection is suspect; it seems much more likely that the tomato was unacceptable because of its color, its vegetable meatiness somehow offensive to the meat- and dairy-focused cuisines of Northern and Central Europe. Indeed, some highly orthodox Jewish sects in Poland initially rejected the tomato because of its "bloodiness"; its red, meaty qualities seemed to violate the sacred sanction against the consumption of blood in any form.

In other parts of the Old World the pattern was much the same. The tomato was accepted and enfolded into cuisines that were based largely on plant foods and that had no pre-existing colorful sauce traditions—the Balkans, the Near and Middle East, sub-Saharan Africa. In other vegetable-centered cultures it was accepted as an addition to the cooking rep-ertoire but did not supplant the already developed richly colored sauce traditions—the soy and curry sauces of Asia and India.

If, then, a large part of the tomato's appeal lies in its color, its ability to evoke richness and meatiness in vegetable form, and to provide visual and gustatory satisfaction to diets low in animal foods, what is ketchup, a tomato-based condiment, doing on our burger? For if all we have hypothesized is valid, then a thick, blood-red sauce would not be predicted as the primary condiment on a hunk of meat. And indeed, it would not be there but for some strange twists that our story has yet to take.

Exported from Mexico to Europe, the tomato returned to

its ancestral home in the New World with Spanish and Portuguese immigrants who settled on the edges of this vast new
territory, an America still in the making. In California, up
from Mexico into the Southwest, along the Gulf of Mexico,
and into the Caribbean, the tomato came back newly fashioned in the traditions of its adopted Mediterranean cuisines,
combined with olive oil and traditional herbs and spices. It
continued as well its original Mexican traditions, flavored with
a variety of chile peppers, with oregano and allspice and
pumpkin seeds, while gradually incorporating a number of
seasoning ingredients introduced by the Spanish—citrus,
cumin, coriander, cinnamon. But these Mexican- and Spanish-
style tomato sauces remained for several centuries on the
fringes of America. The real power structure, the cultural
mainstream, developed on the east coast with colonists from
Western Europe, primarily England, who moved gradually
from east to west across North America, carrying their tastes
and traditions with them. And these were the very people who
had originally rejected the tomato as at best uninteresting and
at worst poisonous.

How were these people seasoning their food? What, if
anything in our European heritage, predisposed or pointed us
in the direction of a sweet and tangy tomato-based condiment
that was to take such a tenacious hold of the American
palate?

The answers lie, surprisingly, not in Europe itself but in

the exotic lands of the Orient, the source from ancient times of the finest, the most expensive, the most coveted, the most flavorful of seasoning ingredients and traditions. Great Britain had established contact with the great spice-producing areas of the Orient—India, Malaysia, the Spice Islands—in the sixteenth and seventeenth centuries through the merchants of the East India Company, who introduced into England many of the spiced and seasoned products of the East. Pickles, relishes, chutneys, condiments, and seasoning sauces crossed the seas on British vessels, no doubt enjoyed by the crews themselves to relieve the monotony of shipboard diet. These products became the basis for a whole new tradition of condiments in England, including sauces like Worcestershire and steak sauce, relishes and pickles like chowchow, piccalilli, and India relish. And although their Oriental forerunners were novel and exotic, complex in their seasonings and their ingredients, these new products were based largely on a long-familiar and basic European seasoning—vinegar. The techniques of Asian flavoring traditions joined established English ingredients to form a whole new set of seasoning and condimental products.

Among these were the ketchups, condimental sauces made from a variety of common English ingredients. The word *ketchup* comes directly from the Indonesian term for soy sauce, *kecap,* and refers more specifically to a dark, viscous, sweetened soy sauce, *kecap manis,* widely used in Indonesian cookery. While the English appropriated the name and the form—that of a strained, darkly colored liquid—they fashioned a distinctly different flavor profile and used it differently. The Indonesian original was based on salted fermented soybeans, sweetened with an unrefined dark sugar that had a faint molasses undertone, and used as a seasoning ingredient in the cooking process. The English namesake was made from widely available local ingredients—primarily walnuts, mushrooms, berries, and grapes—which was tangy with vinegar, lightly sweetened, and used primarily as a condiment on cooked food.

Indeed, although ketchup's name comes from that of Indonesian soy sauce, its English use and ingredients suggest a number of different Asian influences. The piquant tart-sweet flavor of fruits and vegetables and the primary use as a condiment seem more closely related to Indian chutneys than to soy sauce, and the frequent inclusion of anchovies or sardines in many of the ketchups as well as in their sister Worcestershire sauce suggests an affiliation with the fermented fish sauces of Southeast Asia. Whatever the specific influences, it is clear that English ketchups have their origin in the complex flavoring traditions of the Far East and were enthusiastically reshaped and adopted to enhance a diet and a style of cooking that were—for most ordinary people, at any rate—fairly monotonous and unsavory. Although it was a cuisine focused on meat—fish, game, beef, lamb, or mutton—the meat, if experienced at all, was scarce and disappointing; the beef was expensive, the mutton old and gamy. These new piquant condimental sauces added zest and excitement to such imperfect rations.

In addition to salt, vinegar, and mustard, these Asian-inspired tart-sweet ketchups and their related family of condiments and sauces formed the primary seasoning tradition of the English, one that traveled with them when they reached the New World and began their inevitable metamorphosis into Americans. Recipes for mushroom and gooseberry ketchup (frequently called *catsup*) began to appear in eighteenth-century cookbooks; and at the same time that the ketchup tradition was being translated into American terms, the old prejudice against tomatoes was slowly breaking down. Perhaps this change in attitude was due to the influence of some open-minded colonists who recognized the virtues of this versatile and prolific garden crop; perhaps it was the savory evidence of spotty immigrant communities from the Mediterranean, who had long enjoyed the tasty and colorful New World fruit both raw and cooked; perhaps it was Thomas Jefferson, lionized as America's first epicure, who grew tomatoes at Monticello and enjoyed them in a variety of dishes at his cosmopolitan table. Whatever the causes, the tomato was gradually transformed in the eighteenth and nineteenth centuries from a feared and rejected substance into one of the most highly valued crops of the American farm and garden. And this about-face was largely effected by the tomato's incorporation into the ketchup tradition.

A number of factors combined to bring about the felicitous meeting of a new ingredient with an established seasoning practice. First was the American farmsteader's suspicion of anything raw, of foods that were not heavily preserved or thoroughly cooked. Rural folk subsisted largely on flour, cornmeal, and cured pork—ham, sausage, bacon—and turned up their noses at fresh fruit and vegetables, and even, to an extent, at fresh meat. Thomas Jefferson and some "Frenchified" city people might enjoy their "salats" and raw vegetable preparations, but conservative farm people, who made up most of the population, were not at first inclined to eat their tomatoes raw.

Second was the fact that the tomato is a cheap, easily grown, and prolific crop, producing much more than an average family could consume in the limited variety of cooked tomato dishes. This excess made it an obvious choice for preservation as food "put up" for use in winter when no fresh produce was available. Further, while other ethnic traditions, including the original Mexican, treated the tomato as a vegetable, the English regarded it (and correctly so, in botanical terms) as a fruit, sweetening and spicing it in the same way they flavored apples or berries.

Third, and perhaps most important of all, the nineteenth century saw the explosion of refined sugar as a cheap commodity available to everyone on a scale unprecedented in the Western world. The establishment by Europeans of slave-manned sugar cane plantations in the West Indies soon after Columbus's landing led to an industry that would make sweetness in its purest and most intense form affordable and accessible to the masses. Sweetness is a taste that seems to be universally appealing, and the English were particularly enamored of sugar and sweetness in all its forms. Indeed, the English "sweet tooth" had long been observed and commented on by French, Italian, and Spanish visitors, who noted with some disbelief the number of sweetened products in English cookery and the fervor with which they were consumed. Sweet pastries, puddings, jellies and jams, and highly sweetened tea were all routine parts of the common daily diet. This taste for sweet things reached epic proportions in nineteenth-century America with the unleashing of cheap refined sugar into an English-based mainstream fully prepared to indulge its passion.

All of these factors came together at about the same time, and the early years of the nineteenth century saw a proliferation of this exciting new tomato condiment in American farm kitchens. The older traditional ketchups—tart and tangy dark sauces, strained vinegary liquids—became sweeter and thicker, richly red in color. This ketchup was a sauce with body, with great visual appeal, and with a taste that became gradually sweeter as the century progressed. It is interesting to see, in cookbooks of the period, how tomato ketchup developed from its original profile as tangy and highly spiced to less seasoned and highly sweetened; as the sugar went up, the vinegar and the hot peppers went down. And this is, of course, what sugar can do; it is the easiest and most appealing of "cheap" flavors, overwhelming the palate and to a certain extent deadening it to the effect of or need for other more subtle or complex flavors. In 1878 the Heinz Company produced the first commercially bottled ketchup, and it has become the model for the condiment known around the world as America's own.

And it was clearly what America wanted. As we have noted, tomato ketchup was designed at one level to preserve the bountiful harvest of the summer garden for use in winter when no fresh produce was available. Much more significant, however, was its function as an enhancement to monotonous diets, to cured and heavily salted meats that were made tremendously more palatable by the contrasting flavors of the sweet, piquant, colorful sauce. It added zest to fried potatoes, excitement to boiled or baked beans, made bearable the endless round of hashes and croquettes that frugally recycled every last scrap of edible food. And the more we ate it, the more we liked it. Just as other people in other times and other cultures became hooked on the selected seasoning ingredients that gave life and savor to imperfect, boring, or unpalatable foods, Americans got hooked on their own new condiment, to the point where ketchup began to embellish just about everything we ate, providing a familiar, well-loved, and pleasurable taste experience. We had a president who poured it on his "diet" lunch of cottage cheese, and a generation of kids who grew up thinking that Italian food was spaghetti with ketchup on it. And wherever the American GI was sent in the world, the ketchup bottle was sure to follow, providing a reassuring camouflage to unsatisfactory, unfamiliar, or suspect rations.

The rapid success of ketchup and its powerful appeal to the American palate led to the development of a number of other products that had similar characteristics—sweetened, lightly spiced tomato preparations that also became entrenched in the American tradition: Campbell's Tomato Soup, a variety of barbecue sauces, baked beans, salad dressings, and, yes, SpaghettiOs! It was surely the ultimate insult to Gallic sensibilities when early in the century the famous Boston cooking teacher Fannie Farmer stirred some ketchup into a classic vinaigrette and called it "French" dressing, a sweet orange gluey concoction that remains popular—and inappropriately named—to this day. All of these products were spawned from the model of tomato ketchup, which captured the mainstream American palate with a speed and a tenacity that testify eloquently both to the need for added flavor and to a failure of previous ingredients to do the job.

The writer James Fenimore Cooper complained about his

countrymen: "The Americans are the grossest feeders of any civilized nation known. As a nation, their food is heavy, coarse, and indigestible, while it is taken in the least artificial forms that cookery will allow." While this may be a somewhat harsh generalization, there is undoubtedly a great deal of truth in it. The Anglo-American mainstream, like its English predecessor, had little time, incentive, or training in the subtleties and refinements of the culinary arts. Food was hearty, to sate the appetites of hardworking farmers, pioneers, frontiersmen, and cowboys, but it was all too often heavily preserved, greasy, underflavored, and overcooked. For such a diet, ketchup was a godsend, a genuine American innovation, providing both visual and gustatory brightness and excitement, adding an aesthetic dimension to food that was little more than basic nourishment. It is no wonder, then, that we became so quickly attached to it and that it joined the salt and pepper shakers as a basic and pervasive seasoning agent.

The tomato, as a prime component of seasoned sauces, would in our own century finally achieve tremendous popularity through the older but more ethnically marginal cuisines of the Mediterranean, the Southwest, and Mexico. But these sauces, savory rather than sweet, gained their stronghold in the United States decades after ketchup captured the mainstream palate, and the two traditions, the Anglo sweet and the ethnic savory, have existed side by side, occasionally merging and redefining each other. In 1895 Heinz came out with its "chili sauce," an unstrained, somewhat less sweetened version of ketchup, designed as a cooking ingredient, seemingly a mainstream adaptation of the spicy, unsweetened chile sauces of the Southwest. And in 1993, almost a hundred years later, "salsa-style ketchup" made its debut, a response to the growing appreciation of Mexican and Southwestern food by a culture whose taste was firmly rooted in ketchup.

The use of ketchup on the burger was inevitable; by the time the burger made its first major appearance, at around the turn of the century, ketchup had already become entrenched as the primary and most popular of condimental sauces, its appeal to Americans deep and widespread. Its value to other tastes and other traditions is not so all-encompassing; it is accepted and enjoyed for its very "Americanism," its use largely constrained and limited by foods and products experienced and perceived as American in their preparation and presentation.

If, for most of the world, ketchup is defined by its Americanness, it is in large part a characterization that is positive and attractive. For America at its best is a place that has something for everyone, and ketchup as a sauce has something for everyone as well. Like America, it has a complex heritage—the piquant spicy-sweet sauces and relishes of Asia, the tangy vinegars of Western Europe, an exotic, brilliantly colored New World fruit, all mediated by an English passion for sugar and sweetness. But for all this complicated background, ketchup boils down to a sauce that is fairly simple and primal in its appeal. Its thick, smooth texture and rich red color are unprecedented in a world that has long and avidly pursued meaty, full-bodied, highly colored sauces as a vehicle for the enhancement of food. Its sweetness, though not necessarily attractive to everyone, is nonetheless a universally appealing taste, especially to the young, whose preferences historically have never been given much weight but whose culture is paramount in much of the contemporary world. Its spiciness and acidity are toned down to avoid dominating or overwhelming unaccustomed palates, particularly, again, those of the young. It is an easy sauce, the epitome of "cheap" flavor in an unusually attractive garb.

And this is in the end why we love ketchup so much and why the world has come to love it in our name and on our burgers. It represents what we value most in ourselves and what we have cultivated as the best in the American character. It is a friendly, open, no-frills kind of sauce, innovative in a simple, down-home fashion, savvy without being sophisticated. It is unabashedly democratic in its capacity to offer a little something to everyone, to shake hands with the world and not take no for an answer.

Five

THE

VEGGIES

Then a sentimental passion of a vegetable fashion must
  excite your languid spleen,
An attachment à la Plato for a bashful young potato, or
  a not-too-French French bean!
Though the Philistines may jostle, you will rank as an
  apostle in the high aesthetic band,
If you walk down Piccadilly with a poppy or a lily in
  your medieval hand.
              And everyone will say,
              As you walk your flowery way,
"If he's content with a vegetable love which would
  certainly not suit *me*,
Why, what a most particularly pure young man this
  pure young man must be!"

So sang the "fleshly poet" Reginald Bunthorne in Gilbert
and Sullivan's famous operetta *Patience*. It is a spoof of the
mannered and pretentious young literati of the day, using the

vegetable as a metaphor for bloodless and pallid effeminacy. This was a prevalent nineteenth-century English view, one shared by Anglo-America, that vegetables are somehow prissy, effete, without force or vigor—a not uncommon notion, particularly in meat-focused cultures, which equate strength, virtue, and manly fortitude with meat, bloody meat, and disdain the vegetable diet as insubstantial and weak. There is some nutritional basis for this point of view, for most vegetables, excluding the cereal grains and the legumes, are not power-packed with the nutrients necessary to support life; they are, rather, valuable sources of micronutrients like vitamins and minerals, and of dietary fiber, and, as evidence from modern research indicates, they seem to offer a rich variety of disease-fighting compounds. Our mothers and grandmothers may not have had the scientific data to back up their insistence on the healthful benefits of fresh fruits and vegetables, but their beliefs came from a traditional wisdom that included these foods as an important part of the diet.

Despite the fact that vegetables are not for the most part significant sources of basic nourishment and calories provided by protein and fat, they have been around for a long time and have been used as food by humans from the very beginnings of our history. Our earth is, or at least once was, a veritable garden of Eden, a natural salad bar, with thousands of varieties of plants that people found attractive and useful. From this treasure trove humans sampled and experimented, discovering the many parts of different plants that offered a wide variety of eating experiences, from roots, tubers and bulbs, stems and stalks, seeds, berries and fruits, leaves and shoots. Some of these vegetable foods, fleshy tubers like potatoes, yams, and cassava, offered valuable sources of carbohydrates; others contained large amounts of vitamins A and C or were a rich store of such important minerals as iron, calcium, and phosphorous. As we saw in the previous chapter, some vegetables were used not only as food but also as flavoring ingredients; onions, garlic, leeks, and a large number of green herbs, spices, and aromatics are all plant products that are widely used for their seasoning properties, their ability to make the rest of our food taste better. And the many kinds of vegetables growing in different habitats provided a range of flavors, textures, and colors, adding interest and variety to the basic diet.

As we also noted in the chapter on ketchup, fresh vegetables were not very much admired in colonial America, or, indeed, at the end of the nineteenth century, when the hamburger made its first appearance. It is interesting, then, that the current and widely accepted version of the cheeseburger includes a number of vegetables as an important part of its structure. It is a sure indication not only that tastes have changed in America over the last century but that vegetables in general, and this selection of vegetables in particular, have something valuable and desirable to offer across the broad spectrum of human tastes. The veggies that typically appear on the cheeseburger serve, as they have so frequently throughout our history, to highlight the main course, to provide added dimensions of texture, color, and flavor. And they do so in the three basic forms we humans have traditionally chosen to prepare and consume our vegetables—raw, cooked, and preserved.

The raw vegetables that most commonly embellish the cheeseburger are lettuce and tomato, long the standard—and frequently the only—vegetables accepted by Americans in their salads and sandwiches. If the pictorial advertisements of the cheeseburger are to be believed, the lettuce is a delicate fresh green frill, its tender ruffles promising crisp flavorful vegetable goodness. In reality the lettuce is all too often a few thick shreds of a rusty white Styrofoam-like substance, seemingly ancient shards of that American specialty, iceberg lettuce, a solid head that has few nutrients, even less flavor, but a good storage life. It serves some misguided textural function on the cheeseburger, but it has little to do with our ancient, common, and pervasive taste for fresh greens.

Fresh, raw, leafy greens, whether cultivated or wild, have been an important part of the human diet in most parts of the world for a very long time, and for good reason. Most greens contain significant amounts of iron, an essential mineral frequently scarce in many nonmeat foods, as well as calcium, another mineral necessary for the growth and maintenance of bone tissue. Greens are also an extremely rich source of vitamin A, in its precursor carotenes, and may also contain substantial amounts of vitamin C. In addition to these important nutrients, leafy greens provide valuable dietary fiber and offer an interesting variety of textures and flavors, ranging from sweet to mild to bitter to peppery. They may thus have served as a condimental as well as nutritional supplement, making monotonous staple foods more palatable.

Lettuce was cultivated in ancient Egypt, and salads of lettuce and other greens were much appreciated in ancient Greece. Even today, in rural areas of the Aegean, wild greens are collected in the spring and used as a tasty and healthful addition to the basic diet of bread, beans, and olive oil. Ancient Rome also valued lettuce and other leafy greens in a variety of salads; the Roman cookbook writer Apicius offered the following recipe two thousand years ago:

Dress lettuces with vinegar, and a little *liquamen* [salty fish sauce], to make them more easily digestible, to prevent flatulence, and so that the lettuces cannot harm your system.

This recipe is interesting because it offers some insight into the apparently widespread and ancient practice of dressing salads of raw greens with salt and vinegar. Raw greens are particularly susceptible to contamination from human and animal waste because they are eaten neither peeled nor cooked; it is the reason we are advised to avoid salads and other uncooked vegetables when we travel to countries whose standards of hygiene are not ideal. Ancient consumers were undoubtedly no less aware of this problem than we are today; the Chinese, with their long and sophisticated tradition of health and medicine, coupled with a genuine passion for vegetables, have always cooked their greens, if only briefly, in order to prevent microbial infection. Salt and vinegar had been known from very early times to be effective inhibitors of spoilage and decay in food and for this reason were very common and widespread preservative agents. It may be that because they were so effective at preventing harmful effects in one context, they were thought to be equally effective in the context of raw greens; hence the near universal practice of dressing salads with vinegar and salt.

Although the English taste for green salads may have declined in more recent times, earlier traditions show a deep appreciation; this fourteenth-century recipe from the royal household of Richard II contains a rich variety of leafy greens and fresh herbs:

Take parsley, sage, garlic, chibol, onions, leek, borage, mints, porret, fennel, and watercress, rue, rosemary, purslane, laver, and wash them clean. Pick them over, pluck them into small pieces with your hand, and mix them well with raw oil. Add vinegar and salt and serve it forth.

Much as Thomas Jefferson might have relished that salad, his enthusiasm would probably not have been shared by most of his countrymen, with their suspicion and dislike of anything fresh, much less raw. It would not really be until the twentieth century that Americans began truly to appreciate the nutritional benefits and the aesthetic pleasures of raw vegetables, salads, and leafy greens. The repertoire of piquant and flavorful leafy greens, so long a part of the world's tradition, began to expand and proliferate; today's markets stock a variety that would have been unthinkable even twenty or thirty years ago. Still, the mainstream preference for the bland, light-colored, crisp iceberg endures; its presence on the cheeseburger today is evidence, however halfhearted, of a growing American appreciation for a category of vegetable foods that has long been a valued part of the human table.

The second part of the dynamic duo is, of course, the tomato, for in the American culinary lexicon lettuce and tomatoes form as solid a partnership as ham and cheese or bacon and eggs. But while the lettuce has its roots in the Old World, the tomato is a fruit of the New, unknown anywhere outside Central and South America before the Spanish arrived in Mexico in 1519. As we have already seen, many southern European cuisines accepted this new food, enjoying it both cooked into sauces and raw in salads. But Americans remained suspicious; a measure of their resistance is evidenced by the action of a certain Colonel Robert Johnson, who, in 1820, stood on the courthouse steps in Salem, New Jersey, to convince a disbelieving crowd that the consumption of a raw tomato would not cause death on the spot.

Pre-Columbian Mexicans had long used the tomato in conjunction with their beloved chiles in soups, sauces, and spicy salsas; indeed, there is every reason to believe that the tomato functioned in ancient Mexican cuisine in much the same way it does today. Chopped fresh tomatoes were seasoned with chile peppers and salt and used as a spicy, juicy garnish for the basic diet of beans and tortillas. We have appropriated salsa in its traditional form as a delightful condiment for tacos and burritos, but we now use the tomato, sliced rather than chopped, as a flavorful, juicy layer in our own sandwiches. Our breads and fillings may be different from the Mexicans', but we use the tomato to the same effect.

It would be hard to imagine our hoagies, our turkey clubs, our BLTs, without their layer of colorful sliced tomato, but it is in fact a very recent development, occurring in tandem with the burgeoning of the sandwich as a peculiarly American culinary form. It was no doubt motivated in large part by the increasing urbanization of the twentieth century and the need to develop quick, efficient, and attractive lunchtime meals that contained all the elements of a regular meal in one easy package. The salad components of the sandwich meal were the lettuce and the tomato, the standard favorites, now contributing their color, flavor, and texture in a linear, one-bite experience that would ultimately be incorporated into America's favorite sandwich, the cheeseburger. The sliced tomato is our own unique innovation, one that the rest of the world seems to have accepted as an appealing part of the American experience.

So much for the raw veggies—now on to the cooked. Here we may run into a little difficulty, for some of you burger junkies out there will no doubt take issue with my choice of grilled or sautéed onions as the most appropriate. I am well aware that thick slices of raw sweet onion are a popular option, one that I confess to indulging in myself when the first Vidalias of the season make their appearance at the local market. Nor can we disregard the steamed onions that limply garnished the burgers of White Castle, America's first hamburger chain, a form that captured the hearts of a whole generation of consumers. Still, the raw onion and the steamed onion are but variations on the theme; it was fried onions that first embellished the burger and that remain the popular choice.

If there is a single vegetable that can be said to be universal, that vegetable is surely the onion. Along with its odorous relatives garlic, leeks, scallions, shallots, and chives—all members of the lily family—the onion has been eaten by humans for untold thousands of years, serving as both food and flavoring. Eaten raw with bread, onions were the basic food of the pyramid builders of ancient Egypt; the Children of Israel bemoaned the loss of those tasty Egyptian onions and garlic when they fled from bondage to the promised land. The ancient Greeks and Romans valued them in a variety of salads and cooked dishes, and they have always played an important role in much Asian cuisine. The Chinese prefer scallions, which, chopped and stir-fried, add delicate flavor to many dishes. India uses onions, chopped and fried along with garlic and gingerroot, as an essential part of the flavoring of many spiced dishes and curries. And in much of Malaysia and Southeast Asia, small red onions similar to shallots are chopped and deep-fried, to serve as a crisp and flavorful garnish on cooked foods.

Although onions, along with their relatives, have been eaten by all sorts of people throughout the world, they have long had a somewhat unsavory reputation, a taint of commonness and vulgarity. An old Arab tale accounts for their origin by reporting that, when the devil came up to earth from the underworld, onions grew where he first set one foot, garlic where he set the other. Upper-caste Hindus traditionally disdained onions as food unworthy of "respectable" people. Shakespeare admonished his actors not to eat onions or garlic before a performance, and Jonathan Swift penned the following memorable ditty:

There is in every cook's opinion
No savoury dish without an onion:
But lest your kissing should be spoiled
The onion must be thoroughly boiled.

Swift knew what he was talking about; much of the onion's offensive qualities are due to sulfuric compounds produced when the raw flesh is bruised—cut, sliced, or chopped. Released in volatile oils, the noxious compounds irritate the mucous membranes of the eyes, causing tears when onions are chopped. (To prevent this tearing, some sensitive cooks chop onions under cold running water or shield their eyes with a piece of bread held between their teeth.) These compounds are also produced in the mouth when raw onions are chewed, accounting for the notorious "onion breath" or "garlic breath" so widely associated with people less fastidious than ourselves. The effects of this unfortunate condition can last for several hours, as the compounds can get into the bloodstream and are then subsequently expelled from the lungs.

But as cooks have known since time immemorial, cooking tames those pungent fumes, largely doing away with the irritant qualities while retaining the attractive flavoring capacities of the onion. And one of the most enhancing of cooking techniques is the frying or sautéeing of onions in some kind of fat or oil. This process browns or "caramelizes" the natural sugars in the onion, resulting in a product that is soft, sweet, golden brown, and richly flavorful, delicious by itself or as an enhancement to other foods. It is also, of course, one of the most successful techniques for initiating flavor in soups, stews, sauces, and stocks; the preliminary browning of onions in fat is a pervasive technique for flavoring all kinds of cooked food.

In the book *Mastering the Art of French Cooking*, Julia Child, with her colleagues Simone Beck and Louisette Bertholle, wrote: "It is hard to imagine a civilization without onions; in one form or another their flavor blends into almost everything in the meal except the dessert." That there are onions on the cheeseburger should be no surprise; they were widely used in all European cuisines and brought to America by a variety of immigrant cultures. Still, it is German tradition that probably deserves most of the credit for the practice of dressing ground meat with fried onions; it was to prove a happy combination. Onions may be the commonest of common vegetables, but they are also one of the tastiest; they were a fundamental part of the world's table before they became so enduring a part of our own.

As, indeed, were the pickles, those crunchy tangy-sweet slices that are the final vegetable layer in the cheeseburger construction. Pickles are among the oldest of preserved foods, and they occur in remarkably similar forms in cuisines throughout the world. Their widespread use and appeal testify not only to peoples' need to store or preserve plentiful foods for times of scarcity but also to the aesthetic value those products provide. Modern technology has assured that we no longer have to smoke our salmon or corn our beef or pickle our okra; we can have the finest and freshest pretty much whenever we please. And yet we continue to enjoy and to covet these preserved foods and frequently pay a good deal more for them than for their fresh equivalents. What began in older and simpler times as a practical concern for preserving valuable food resources seems to end up inevitably as a gastronomic experience, the pleasure and delight we derive from traditional and familiar forms of food preparation.

In their long history people have preserved a number of different foods, including meat, fish, eggs, vegetables, and fruits. Cheese, as we have already noted, is a form of preserved milk. And a variety of preservative techniques developed in preindustrial times to fit the demands of different food substances in different climatic and geographic circumstances. Drying, smoking, salting, and pickling are all venerable techniques and all produce very striking sensory changes in the foods they affect. Because these preserved foods are so dramatically transformed in terms of their sensory and gustatory impact, they take on a culinary life of their own, providing a whole new range of eating experiences. Grapes that have been dried, and thus preserved, turn into something new and wholly different; raisins are not only far less perishable but they also offer a brand-new range of possibilities for cooking and eating.

Pickles are no different, for whether the food is animal or vegetable, the pickling process produces dramatic changes. These are due to the effects of the two primary pickling agents, salt and acid. There are two basic ways to make pickles. The first is a fermentative process in which the vegetables are placed in a salt brine strong enough to prevent the growth of unwanted microorganisms but weak enough to encourage the growth of certain bacteria that produce lactic acid. Frequently the fermentation is aided by some kind of grain product; the Japanese use a rice bran mash to ferment their pickles, and Eastern Europeans may use a hunk of rye bread to facilitate the process. This fermentative pickling technique is the one used to produce sauerkraut and many of the sour pickles of both Europe and Asia. The second, and most common, way to make pickles is to salt the vegetables in order to draw out the liquid in the tissues, then cover the vegetables with vinegar, to which flavorings such as sugar, herbs, and spices may be added. In both techniques it is the acid that penetrates the tissues of the vegetables and preserves them from spoilage. But in spite of the two constant ingredients—salt and acid—pickles can vary widely because of differences in the nature and length of the pickling process, and in the seasoning ingredients added to the pickling liquid.

This salty acid bath is also called a "pickle"; the expression "to be in a pickle" means to be awash in a difficult situation from which there is no obvious escape. And "to be pickled" means to have one's own tissues saturated, not with pickle juice but with alcohol.

Pickles, like other preserved foods, frequently transcend their more practical function and become hooked into the aesthetics of any culinary tradition. Wherever you may go in the world, you will find that people are extremely attached to their own pickles and are very dependent on them to provide savor and zest to certain foods and certain meals. A slice of French country pâté is far less appealing without its accompanying crock of *cornichons,* those sour little bites that provide such a welcome complement to the rich, fatty meat. And who can imagine a corned beef sandwich without the tangy foil of a half-sour dill?

The Japanese are passionate pickle lovers, delighting in pickles of such vegetables as daikon, turnip, eggplant, cucumber, and gingerroot, the tastes ranging from mild to sweet to strongly sour and tangy. They are eaten throughout the meal and are frequently consumed as a final course, a kind of *digestif* to settle the stomach and aid digestion. Indeed, in this respect, pickles seem to function cross-culturally; the odd but widely reported craving for pickles by pregnant women occurs in China as well as America, and may attest to the nausea-quelling, stomach-settling properties of strong salty-sour tastes. On the other hand, Hungarian women traditionally drank pickle juice as an aid to the complexion, so who knows what other wonders this humble preserve can work?

The rest of Asia, in addition to Japan, is a treasure-house of pickles, from the tangy, chile-spiced mustard greens and cabbage of Szechuan to the lime and mango pickles of India, some of them highly sweetened and spiced with ginger, garlic, cinnamon, cloves, and mustard seeds. Korean cuisine has given us that mouth-exploding marvel kimchi, fermented cabbage spiked with chile peppers. Kimchi is thought to be the ancestor of our more familiar sauerkraut, originally introduced into Germany by Mongol tribes who penetrated Eastern Europe as far as the Danube.

The Middle East has a rich pickle tradition, involving onions, peppers, string beans, cucumbers, and eggplant, and the entire Mediterranean is an ancient hearth of cured and salted olives, to many minds the most sublime form of preserved vegetables; the region has also given us those eccentric, piquant pickled buds of the caper bush. The rest of Europe has its own venerable traditions, pickling such common vegetables as beets, cabbage, and cucumbers, flavored with garlic and dill, bay leaves and mustard seeds.

All these many varieties, a veritable plethora of pickles, were once produced in individual homes by individual cooks or pickle makers, each producer and each region taking pride in the unique and savory virtues of a distinctive product.

Nowadays in most of the world pickles are commercially produced and widely available. There is, however, nothing like a homemade pickle to evoke nostalgia, to conjure up sweet memories of food lovingly put up at home, of a bountiful summer harvest preserved for the lean winter months.

I know, because I grew up with a grandmother who was overcome with pickle madness once a year, every year, for as long as I can remember. This grandma, whose ancestors had come from Germany several generations before she was born, was an urban middle-class person who had lived her entire life in Brooklyn, New York, in the shadow of Ebbetts Field; she never planted a garden and she never, as far as I know, set foot upon a farm. Yet once a year, without fail, in the second or third week of August, this otherwise unerratic woman was seized by a frenzy that was not to be denied, an obsessive need to preserve cucumbers. Those vegetables came not from someone's backyard plot but from the corner grocer, whose cucumber bins she ransacked, without a care to size, age, or regularity of appearance. When the job was done, her pickling passion spent, there stood six gallon-sized jars on the kitchen table, enough to last us through yet one more interminable year. For, alas, Grandma was a terrible cook, her lack of skill matched only by a palate unable to assess any culinary deficiencies. Her pickles were the worst I have ever eaten. Soft and slimy from overprocessing, tinted a piercing chartreuse from an overdose of turmeric, they floated like jellyfish in a urine-colored brine awash with mustard seeds. The seeds, if not the pickles, provided a certain redemptive pleasure, for when adult backs were turned, we grandchildren would scoop gobs of them from the pickle jar and spit them at one another, with a speed and accuracy that improved from year to year.

I now understand my grandma's pickle mania as an atavistic urge, latent in all of us, to put away food for times of scarcity, as once our ancestors must surely have done. It is a primal call in the blood and the brain, a throwback to a time when we were more directly and more intimately involved with our food, with the growing and cooking and preserving and planning, when we and the food that nourished us were more closely connected to the rhythms and realities of the natural world. Pickles, perhaps more than any other preserved product, have the capacity to evoke, with a palpable tang, that collective memory of times long past. And so we haunt the pickle barrels on the Lower East Side and canvas the displays at state fairs, where bread-and-butters and icebergs and Polish dills seduce us still with their siren songs of vinegar and salt.

America is heir to a whole world of pickles and she has done proud by her legacy. We have always been a nation of pickle lovers, beginning with the early colonists, who brought with them their pickling traditions from the Old World. On these shores they met up with a bright new range of possibilities—the corn, the green tomatoes, the peppers, both hot and sweet, that were the native products of this New World—and other fruits and vegetables brought in by different groups of people, like okra and watermelon from Africa. These many new foods entered into a burgeoning and innovative American tradition that, at the end of the nineteenth century, turned into a productive commercial enterprise. A quick stroll down the condiment aisle gives ample testimony: midgets, gherkins, spears, and chunks; mixed pickles, sweet pickles, sour pickles, hot pickles; onions, olives, eggplant, watermelon rind. It is a wealth and variety that are truly astonishing, that might even have stopped Grandma in her tracks—but somehow I don't think so!

The pickles on our cheeseburger are about as mainstream American as any, and, like so many of the other seasoning and condimental products of the Anglo-American tradition, they are frequently sweetened. Like ketchup, the sweet pickle came to America from England and to England from India via the East India Company, a descendant of the spiced sweet and sour pickles, relishes, and chutneys of Indian cuisine. Its sweet spicy flavor is very different from that of most other European pickles, with their predominantly salty-sour pucker, and although the sour pickle continues to be very popular, associated with specific foods and certain ethnic traditions, it is the sweet pickle that has come to be emblematic of American taste. Once again, the notorious English sweet tooth and the availability of cheap refined sugar combined to produce flavors and products that were immensely appealing. Even other immigrant groups, like the Germans, for example, whose pickle tradition from the Old World was solidly based on the salty-sour flavor profile, enthusiastically accepted the new sweetened pickles while retaining the old traditional favorites. The Pennsylvania Dutch practice of "seven sweets and seven sours," a variety of condimental accessories to the main meal, was one that developed here in America as an amalgam of old and new pickling and seasoning traditions.

It is fitting, and not surprising, that our favorite pickle is a cucumber pickle, for although we produce and enjoy a wide variety of pickled fruits and vegetables, it is the cucumber that is a near universal choice. A prolific grower in both temperate and tropical environments, it retains its attractive crunch and crispness and absorbs gracefully the decisive flavors that pickling prescribes. It is cultivated in a variety of types and sizes, from the tiny *cornichon* to the dainty midget gherkins to the tough old survivors of the backdoor garden, traditional denizens of the pickle barrel. It can be pickled whole, sliced in a number of different ways, or chopped into mixed vegetable hashes known as pickle relishes.

There are some aficionados who dress up their burgers with pickle relish rather than pickle slices. This is, to my mind, a mistake, because the slices provide a textural layer that the relish cannot; its thick soupy consistency is too close in texture to that of the ketchup, reducing if not eliminating one of the important sensations that occur in every bite. There is also a product called "hamburger relish," which combines pickle relish and ketchup in one bottle, and though it has its misguided adherents, it blurs the lines and blunts the total sensory experience of the ideal cheeseburger.

The four vegetables—lettuce, tomatoes, onions, and pickles—complete the structure of the cheeseburger as a whole meal-in-the-hand, with salad, veggies, and condiments. Their presence reinforces the long and widely held view of vegetables as attractive and important additions to the human diet, elements that are of clear nutritional and aesthetic value. Not only do vegetables provide dietary fiber and a number of essential vitamins and minerals not found in animal foods or grain products but they offer as well a refreshing variety of flavors, colors, and textures that add interesting new dimensions to our basic foods. They may not be the center of the meal, but they are crucial accessories, dressing up the same old stuff with sparkle and style. We have, all of us, an age-old and intense involvement with plant foods, and the cheeseburger's selection, intrinsic to the American tradition, gives at least a passing nod to our universal vegetable passion.

Six

THE
FRENCH
FRIES

*O*f the many components of the cheeseburger platter, with their diverse culinary and linguistic roots in a variety of cultures and cuisines from the Old World to the New, only the french fries have a clear national designation, one that has never been contested. The golden crisp deep-fried potato strips that are so fundamental a part of the American experience are acknowledged here as well as throughout the world as a Gallic invention, only one of the numerous offspring that resulted from the happy marriage of a New World tuber with French culinary expertise. But even though the french fry was invented in France and remains to this day intrinsic to that nation's table, it is America that in just the last century provided it with its most appreciative audience. The french fry is the single most popular "fast" food in the country and is well on its way to achieving a similar level of success throughout the rest of the world.

Who could have known that the homely starchy tuber discovered by the Spanish in the highlands of Peru would come to be such a desirable food for so many people in so many different parts of the world? The potato seems at first glance an unlikely candidate for stardom, with its bumpy, irregular appearance, its variety of sometimes unattractive skin colors, its habit of growing underground. Yet the potato had been cultivated as a staple food in its ancient Andean hearth for many thousands of years, providing an essential dietary resource in areas where the known cereal grains, primarily maize, could not easily be grown. The Incan *papa* (the ancient Quechua name has been retained in the Spanish word for "potato") was a non-finicky grower, tolerating both heat and cold, dampness and aridity, requiring minimum cultivation, and easily propagated from seed or, more commonly, from the planting of potato "eyes." The starchy tubers, with their large stores of carbohydrate, as well as such valuable nutrients as potassium and vitamin C, were a life-sustaining crop in geographic and climatic areas where other crops could not succeed and animal resources were scarce.

South American culinary traditions for preparing the potato do not seem to have included frying; perhaps if they had, the potato might have enjoyed an even more rapid success in Europe than it did. Incan practice seems to have revolved around cooking the tubers in liquid, in soups and stews, or baking them in the hot ashes of the hearth fire. Pre-Columbian potato specialists also developed a process for freeze-drying, a not unlikely discovery in the peculiar climatic conditions of the Andes, with their freezing nights and warm dry days. Sliced potatoes were spread out at night to freeze, then trampled (or pounded) and dried during the day. After many days of alternate freezing and drying, a product called *chuño* was obtained, a compact dehydrated form of potato that could be stored for long periods without spoilage, ensuring a supply of food when the fresh vegetables were not available. The finest grades of *chuño* were milled into a kind of flour used to make bread.

After its introduction into Europe by the Spanish in the early decades of the sixteenth century, the potato was largely rejected as unfit for consumption by humans and was used primarily as food for livestock. But it was disdained for the most part by people who could afford to disdain it, who had access to animal foods and satisfactory supplies of cereal grains. The poor of Europe, particularly those of Northern and Eastern Europe, were not so fastidious when it came to a choice between ongoing malnutrition and an unfamiliar vegetable capable of sustaining life. The Irish, in particular, with a difficult climate and a land long ravaged by war, accepted the nourishing, good-natured, easy-growing potato with gratitude; within fifty years of its introduction near the end of the sixteenth century, it became the central and crucial focus of Irish cuisine, supplanting the difficult and frequently disappointing grain crops that had previously fed the poor. So successful was the potato in nourishing the Irish that it achieved a reputation elsewhere as a potent aphrodisiac, the reasoning being that eating lots of potatoes resulted in lots of Irish babies! Unfortunately, the Irish dependence on the potato would ultimately prove catastrophic: When the potato blight struck in 1845, it resulted in mass starvation, disease, and death, and thus initiated the first great emigration of the Irish to America.

The potato took somewhat longer to be accepted in other areas, but eventually the virtues of this cooperative, pleasant, and filling tuber were recognized by much of Eastern and Northern Europe; by the end of the eighteenth century the potato was solidly entrenched as a dietary staple in Germany, Poland, Russia, Scandinavia, and the Low Countries. It was these cuisines, along with the traditions of Irish and English potato eaters, that would ultimately provide the foundations for early American potato cookery.

In France the acceptance of the potato was effected largely by Antoine-Auguste Parmentier, an eighteenth-century agronomist who, as a prisoner of war in Prussia, had lived for several years on a steady diet of potatoes, and who recognized the value of this vegetable as a cheap, satisfying, and nourishing food. He demonstrated to the French how the potato could be easily and deliciously adapted into existing culinary practice, and so great were his passion and his dedication that within a couple of generations the potato had become fully enfolded into French cuisine. Early in the nineteenth century,

Brillat-Savarin wrote in his treatise on gastronomy: "We understand by starch the flour or dust that may be obtained from cereal grains, leguminous plants, and from many sorts of roots, amongst which the potato holds the first rank at the present day." Potato starch, to which Brillat-Savarin referred, was initially (and unsuccessfully) introduced to the French as an alternative to wheat or rye flour for bread, but it was as a vegetable that the potato would ultimately find its place of honor in the French kitchen.

We don't know the name of the French genius who first thought to toss some strips or slices of potato into a kettle of boiling oil or fat (actually, he or she may well have been Belgian), but it probably occurred sometime in the latter decades of the eighteenth century. Deep-frying potatoes seems to have become standard practice by 1839, for it is in that year that the French take credit for the invention of *pommes soufflés,* those ethereal golden crispy puffs that result when deep-fried potatoes are partially cooked in hot oil, then removed and refried at a higher temperature. It is likely, at any rate, that the deep-frying of potatoes, as well as of other foods, was popularized as a public or restaurant practice; large vessels of boiling oil or fat were not a commonplace feature of the domestic kitchen.

Although Thomas Jefferson, with his great admiration for all things French, is said to have obtained a recipe for french fries in 1802, it would be another hundred years or so before the french fry achieved its tremendous popularity in America. This seems to have happened after World War I, when American soldiers who had been stationed in France and the Low Countries brought back with them a deep affection for the product as well as the name by which it would henceforth be known.

Deep-frying, however, was not a common practice for many of those people who constituted the mainstream of early America—the English, the Germans, the Dutch, and, later, the Irish. These people were all dedicated potato eaters and had brought with them from their European homes already well-established traditions of potato cookery. All of these traditions involved the use of fat—fat for garnishing, fat for enriching, fat for pan-frying. From the English and the Irish, for example, came the popular practice of boiling and mashing potatoes, then enriching them with butter, cream, or buttermilk, or of shaping leftover mashed potatoes into cakes or croquettes that were then fried in butter or meat drippings. German tradition favored potatoes pan-fried with onions in bacon fat, then seasoned with salt and vinegar, a recipe that in America was refashioned as German hot potato salad. The Dutch frequently made a whole meal of boiled potatoes (two pounds per person) speared from a common bowl and then dipped into cups of warm fat; these sturdy Hollanders were also fond of pureed potatoes topped with fried bacon and plenty of bacon fat. Later, new immigrants from Scandinavia and Eastern Europe would contribute their potato traditions, with recipes that also used butter, bacon fat, and, of course, sour cream.

What all these preparations have in common is a heavy and intensive use of fat in conjunction with potatoes, fat that is used both as a cooking medium and as an enriching and enhancing additive. And the fat is all animal fat, whether in the form of dairy products (butter, milk, cream) or rendered meat fat (bacon fat, drippings, lard). Here we have a basic vegetable carbohydrate food eaten not by itself but with the constant addition of another substance that seems to make it more palatable. Does the description ring a bell? The pervasive practice of cooking and eating potatoes with fat looks curiously similar to the practice we discussed earlier—that of beefing up grain- or plant-based diets with highly seasoned sauces and strong flavoring ingredients.

The fact is that the potato traditions of Northern Europe, which were to become the basis of subsequent American practice, use fat as a kind of condimental agent, providing both nutritional and gastronomic enrichment. A steady diet of potatoes—starchy, mealy, bland—would prove as unsatisfactory as plain boiled rice or plain corn tortillas or plain millet porridge, without the addition of some other ingredients that enhance the flavor and, if possible, supplement and round out the nutritional profile of a single staple plant food. And Northern Europe, with its meat- and dairy-focused cultures, had long used fat to provide that crucial finishing-off, to make monotonous bland vegetable foods go down easier. While other cuisines use spices and seasonings to accomplish this, those who have it use fat. The need and the structure are the same; it is only the ingredients that differ.

This practice is extremely widespread and finds eloquent expression in many diverse cultures. The Bemba, a traditional Bantu people from northern Rhodesia, have long subsisted on a thick millet porridge called *ubwali,* a very stiff mixture that is scooped from the bowl and rolled with the fingers into a ball. The ball is then dipped into a tasty sauce or relish called *umunani,* a kind of liquid stew made from a variety of ingredients—bits of meat, ants, caterpillars, vegetables, peanuts, and seasoning. Although the Bemba regard the millet porridge as essential to the meal and do not feel that they have been adequately fed unless they have eaten *ubwali,* they also feel that they cannot eat the *ubwali* without the accompanying *umunani.* The seasoned sauce makes the porridge balls "slide down the throat," allowing the thick glutinous starch to go down easier. And there is no question that it also makes the food taste better, adding zest and variety to an otherwise bland and monotonous diet.

The *ubwali–umunani* system maintained by the Bemba is strikingly similar to a dietary principle long espoused by the Chinese, although the Chinese account for it in somewhat different terms. Chinese philosophy rests on a strong belief in balance and harmony in all things—the yin-yang—and food is no exception. A meal that presents a balance of elements is not only pleasing and enjoyable for the palate but also appropriately nourishing, creating a harmony between body and spirit. The dietary principle that describes this balance is called *fan-ts'ai,* and it divides food into two basic categories: *fan,* which is the basic grain or starch food, and *ts'ai,* which is a variety of dishes made from other ingredients that are a necessary complement to *fan. Fan* can be rice or noodles or porridge or dough in any form, while *ts'ai* comprises an extraordinary variety of preparations made from, for example, meat, seafood, bean curd, or vegetables, cooked and flavored with any number of seasoning ingredients. While *fan* is the central and more important component, without which no meal is a meal, *ts'ai* is necessary to balance, to complement, to round out the whole. (The American experience of Chinese food shows how little we understand the system; when we order dinner in a Chinese restaurant we concentrate on the *ts'ai* foods and look upon the *fan* as a secondary or side dish.) Like the Bemba, the Chinese system illustrates the importance, both dietary and aesthetic, of providing variety, flavor, and richness to basic grain or carbohydrate diets. From the nutritional point of view, a meal consisting solely of grains or starches represents an imbalance, as from the aesthetic point of view monotony is an imbalance. Once again imperfect foods require some additional supplement or embellishment to make them more acceptable and more pleasing to their human consumers.

The garnish, of course, can take many forms. The Bemba eat their millet balls with wild mushrooms or stewed locusts or savory groundnut sauces, while the Chinese may complement their rice with bits of chicken and vegetables in a spicy black bean sauce, or may stuff a wheat-dough dumpling wrapper with shredded cabbage and pork. Italians dress their pasta with rich sauces of garlic and herbs, tomatoes and olive oil, while the Thais eat rice with spicy curries made of coconut and fish sauce, chile peppers and fresh coriander. The garnish can be a complex composition of bits of meat or seafood, vegetables, and seasonings, or it can be a simple sauce made of one or two ingredients. It often uses some fat or oil, if only at times in very small amounts, and the very poorest people, like many in India, may be able to afford nothing more than a handful of chopped chiles to dress up the rice. Whatever the varieties of culinary expression, so dependent on history and geography, traditions and resources, the practice remains constant and consistent across cultures.

In most of Europe the supplement to the traditional grain or starch dishes, in the form of bread, pasta, or porridges, was animal fat. The fat varied from region to region and culture to culture; in areas of intensive beef and dairy traditions, like France and the British Isles, the supplement was more heavily in the form of beef suet, beef tallow, meat drippings, and dairy products, while in areas more strongly dependent on pork the supplement was likely to be in the form of lard or bacon fat. Jews from Eastern Europe, forced by the constraints of their religion to avoid the pork products so prevalent in that region, turned to rendered goose or chicken fat to provide their condimental or cooking fat. And there was, of course, a good deal of crossover; most of these cultures had dairy products as well as animal fats, and used butter and cream and cheese to enrich their grain dishes. These practices have all become an enduring part of the American experience. We butter our bread, our pancakes, our oatmeal, and even our corn on the cob, that novel unfamiliar grain we encountered when we came as immigrants to this New World. We enrich our vegetables, our soups, and our bean dishes with bacon and salt pork; we eat macaroni with cheese sauce. Hungarian-Americans still butter their noodles and Jewish Americans still spread *schmalz* on their rye bread. The conditions that spawned these practices may no longer be relevant, but the dishes and products that resulted are hooked into our traditions, now familiar, pleasurable, and well-loved foods.

When the potato was introduced into Europe, it was enfolded into these very same fat-enriched starch or grain traditions, and the resulting dishes were brought to America to become the basis of the potato recipes we enjoy today— boiled, baked, or mashed potatoes enriched with butter, cream, or sour cream; scalloped potatoes baked with milk and cheese; potatoes cooked in the drippings of roasting meat; potatoes pan-fried in bacon fat; potato cakes and potato latkes sautéed in butter or chicken fat. And America would contribute her own unique innovation—potato salad—that (sometimes) marvelous concoction of cold boiled potatoes mixed with onions, celery, and mayonnaise, yet another way of enriching the starchy tuber with a savory fat substance.

But the french fry remained an elusive latecomer, for a couple of good reasons. First, deep-frying was not a common home kitchen technique; it requires a great deal of oil or fat and it is fairly messy, producing unpleasant fumes and a hard-to-clean buildup of grease. And the constant high heat necessary to produce properly fried foods is difficult to regulate. Still, fried foods had some impact on the early American tradition. Dutch housewives fried round cakes of dough in fat; Washington Irving described them as "balls of sweetened dough fried in hog's fat and called dough nuts or oly koeks [oily cakes]." The South developed an extensive repertoire of fried foods, perhaps because the kitchens, manned by slaves, were frequently out of doors or separated from the main living quarters. Battered deep-fried chicken—known to this day as southern fried chicken—cornmeal-crusted fish, and hush puppies, those crunchy golden fried nuggets of seasoned cornmeal batter, were all southern specialties that remain popular traditional foods.

The second reason that french fries may have been so late in making their appearance is that deep-frying was a technique long associated with dough-wrapped foods or those dipped in batter. This is so because frying at high temperatures works most successfully on foods with a high starch content; the compact starch molecules slowly expand in the hot oil or fat, allowing the inner portion of the food to cook while the outer surface browns and becomes crisp. Less starchy foods like chicken or fish simply dry out and burn, without maintaining the inner moistness and juiciness that make properly fried foods so palatable. It is for this reason that deep-fried foods are customarily wrapped in some sort of dough—like an egg roll or a samosa—or coated in a starchy batter made from some variety of cereal flour. At the same time the hot oil or fat cooks the inner food, it caramelizes or browns the natural sugars in the coating, producing the attractive golden color and the typical appealing flavor compounds that are characteristic of fried foods. While all these complicated processes are going on, the liquid content of the dough or batter is cooked away, resulting in a crisp and crunchy coating. And that savory, crisp golden exterior is yet another flag that signals "fat," something that people throughout the world respond to.

The Chinese have a long popular tradition of fried street or snack foods, a dazzling variety of fritters, puffs, pancakes, egg rolls, pastries, and turnovers; crisp-coated tidbits of seafood, vegetables, and bean curd; and savory mixtures of ground or shredded meat and vegetables. Wheat flour frequently makes up the dough or batter, but rice flour and cornstarch are also commonly used.

The Japanese have not traditionally utilized deep-frying to any great extent, but they have surely made an art of tempura, said to have been introduced by the Portuguese in the sixteenth century. Tempura, properly executed, is a high point in deep-frying—bits of seafood and artfully sliced vegetables coated with a delicate batter, quickly fried to a lacy crunch, then dipped into gingery soy sauces. Tempura is the Japanese counterpart of the Indian *pakora*, chunks and slices of different vegetables coated with a seasoned batter made of wheat or chickpea flour and deep-fried to a spicy golden crispness. India too maintains a rich tradition of dough-wrapped and battered fried foods—pancakes, turnovers, and pastries, stuffed with a variety of savory fillings and served with sweet and spicy relishes and chutneys.

One thing worth observing about this variety of deep-fried foods is that the enriching with fat, which occurs through the medium of a crisp starch coating, is used almost exclusively in conjunction with fairly lean foods. Seafood, poultry (primarily chicken), vegetables, and (like hush puppies) bits of batter itself are the foods traditionally enhanced with deep-frying. Red meats are almost never prepared in this way, perhaps because, as we noted in the chapter on meat, they carry their own load of fat and rarely need further enriching. The one exception to this general common practice is that bizarre concoction known as chicken-fried steak, a dish popular in the American West. It consists of slices of beef, usually tough and of fairly poor quality, thickly battered and deep-fried, and then served smothered with a bland white cream gravy. It violates so many widely held notions of appropriate culinary practice and taste that I am certain it was a plateful of the stuff that inspired James Fenimore Cooper to denounce American cooking as "coarse, heavy, undigestible, and greasy."

Because traditions of deep-frying revolve around coated foods, the potato does not at first seem an obvious choice. And yet, as it turns out, it has the ideal composition for the practice. Like the high-starch semiliquid batters that provide the perfect coating material for foods that are to be fried, the potato is itself a high-starch substance with enough water in its tissues to permit the fullest realization of deep-frying. No intermediary coating or wrapping is required; immersed in boiling oil or fat, properly sliced potatoes achieve the exemplary form of a deep-fried food. The outer surfaces are instantly sealed and slowly browned, with all the flavor, color, and crispness that fried starch provides, while the inside portion is cooked to a melting softness. The result offers the textural pleasure of crispness and softness in each golden bite.

What we have with the french fry is a near perfect enactment of the enriching of a starch food with oil or fat. As opposed to the fat's being added to a cooked food—as, for example, when we put a pat of butter or a dollop of sour cream on a baked potato—the fat is provided by the cooking technique itself. Pan-frying or sautéeing does the same thing, of course, but the gastronomic result is very different: The product is uneven or irregular in its brownness and crispness, and much of the cooking fat is absorbed, while with deep-frying the hot fat seals, cooks, and browns without being absorbed by the food. The french fry, properly executed, provides an ideal interaction between substance (starch), medium (fat or oil), and technique (high heat immersion), resulting in a product that is uniform in all its sensory attributes—the characteristic flavor, aroma, color, and texture of fried foods that are so widely appealing.

Of course, the operative words here are *properly executed,* for as with all culinary products and practices, there are rules and cautions to be observed in the pursuit of the perfect french fry. The oil or fat must be maintained at a constant high temperature, ideally between 370° and 380°F. If the oil is too hot, it will burn the outside surface of the potato strips before the inside is fully cooked, and if the temperature is too low, the cooking time will increase and more grease will be absorbed. The type of oil or fat is a matter of some dispute; before certain vegetable oils were widely available, animal fats like lard or beef tallow were commonly used for deep-frying, and both produce very savory fried foods. Because of current health issues, however, such animal fats are in disrepute and are no longer widely used, even though the flavors they produce are considered superior to those produced by most oils. (The recent debate about vegetable oil versus beef tallow in some of the fast-food franchises' french fries reflects the ongoing and escalating tension between a concern for better health and a desire for the tastiest possible food.) Any oil or fat used in the deep-frying process should have a high smoke point, the temperature at which the oil breaks down and produces smoke and noxious fumes. Olive and sesame oils have relatively low smoke points and are therefore inappropriate for deep-frying, while peanut and cottonseed oils have much higher smoke points and are therefore more suited to frying at high temperatures.

Most experts agree that the proper potato for french frying is a mealy, nonwaxy type, best represented in this country by the common Idaho baking potato. The reason for this choice is not simply a textural issue: Waxy potatoes contain a higher proportion of sugar than mealy potatoes, and sugar caramelizes or browns much more quickly than starch. A potato with too much sugar will brown too quickly on the surface before the inside is properly cooked. The issue of starch is also invoked in the common practice of soaking the uncooked sliced potatoes in water before they are fried, supposedly to soak out excess starch. In fact it is starch that is responsible for the attractive browning of the potato. Soaking in water may still be desirable, however, so that when the potato is plunged into boiling oil it does not dehydrate too quickly.

Finally there is the issue of the size and shape of the potato cuts, an area thoroughly muddied by the food industry's recent proliferation of frozen french fries in an unseemly variety of sizes and shapes—thick, thin, round, long, crinkled, curlicued, waffled, twisted, even shaped into the letters of the alphabet. The quest for novelty and variety leads in this case to products that are unique visually but unsatisfactory gustatorily, their over-elaborated shapes providing too much surface for the absorption of fat. The straight slender strip remains the classic—Escoffier stipulated a half-inch cut, thin but not so thin that it becomes crisp all the way through before the outside attains its perfect golden sheathing. This having been stated, I must now confess that the best french fry I ever ate was a good deal thicker than the prescribed ideal, a genuine regional variant produced by the original Nathan's in Coney Island some forty years ago—thick, crisp, and darkly brown, with a melting succulent inside that could seduce the most exacting epicure. It remains the best of what was, an unextinguishable salivatory memoir of childhood.

In his book *The Physiology of Taste*, Brillat-Savarin wrote:

Fried foods are always welcome in entertainments; they introduce a pleasing variety, they are agreeable to look

at, they keep their original savour, and can be eaten by
the hand, which always pleases ladies.

Published shortly before his death in 1826, the treatise dealt
with the general category of fried foods and not with the fried
potato, with which he seems not to have been familiar. But
what Brillat-Savarin observed about other fried foods applies
at least as well to the potato—a savory appealing food that
can be eaten with the hands. And if it was only "ladies" in
eighteenth-century France who appreciated the special pleasures of finger food, that is certainly not the case today, when
the french fry is enthusiastically gobbled up by ladies and just
about everyone else. One of the reasons is surely that, like
the burger, it provides that delightful intimacy with our food
that seems to be so universally attractive. But unlike the
burger, with its appeal to our atavistic desire to cram our
mouths with meat, juice, and fat, the french fry offers a more
refined and sophisticated experience of pick-uppable food.
The slender, almost dainty strips, with their crisp dry exterior, encourage contact without contamination, except, perhaps, for those final clinging salt crystals that we sensuously
lick from our fingers.

The french fry may well be civilization's most satisfactory
realization of the enhancing of starch with fat, a product that
was created only when the near perfect substance, the potato,
made its way from its provincial birthplace in South America

to the center of a more universal stage. It is not without irony that this potato, transformed by Gallic tradition, would be introduced once again to the world from its adopted North American home, this time in a far more widely attractive form. A good portion of the world may not relish baked potatoes with sour cream or scalloped potatoes with butter and cheese or boiled potatoes ladled with bacon fat. But the french fry is a universal favorite because it offers all the positive attributes of a fat-enriched vegetable in one simple and complete package. All the unique and desirable characteristics of fried food—the savory flavor and aroma, the golden color, the crisp exterior surrounding a soft melting center—are presented in an easy toothsome finger-held bite. The potato may have fulfilled its nutritional destiny as a valuable belly-filler for the masses, but in its role as the french fry it has given us very much more of what we value in our food—sensory pleasure, playfulness, and the charm of fat in its perhaps most elegant form.

Seven

THE
SOFT
DRINK

We have regaled ourselves thus far with a variety of solid foods—the burger with its melting cheese and savory garnishes, the crispy golden french fries—so by now we long for a little liquid refreshment. And there it is, ready to hand, bubbling in an attractive red cup, its icy effervescence an invitation and a promise of pleasures yet unexplored. The Coke, along with its extended family of flavored, colored, carbonated soft drinks, is surely one of the oddest substances devised by humankind, and yet it reveals, on closer inspection, many of the same patterns and preferences characteristic of our solid food. Our species is no less inclined, it would seem, to manipulate its liquid intake than it is to transform its solid, producing novel foods and drinks unprecedented in the natural world. And though the Coke is just as thoroughly American in its history and presentation as the rest of our cheeseburger meal, its appeal clearly transcends any particular national origins. What is it about this unique beverage that makes it so attractive to so many different people, and what if anything is there in the evolution of our liquid consumption that leads to this particular sweet, cold, bubbly drink?

Like all animals, humans need water; indeed, water is second in importance only to oxygen as an element necessary to sustain life. We can survive for weeks without food of any kind, and for months and even years without certain essential nutrients, but without water we die within days. This is because water performs a number of vital functions in the body's regulation and maintenance and must constantly be replenished in order to do its job properly. Water makes up between fifty to seventy percent of body weight in humans; it acts as the medium through which nutrients are carried to the cells and wastes and impurities removed. It lubricates the joints, is an essential ingredient in the absorption and digestion of food, and supplies the critical fluid medium in which all chemical changes take place. A good deal of the body's fluids are lost or used up each day through the evacuation of wastes in the urine and feces, through normal breathing, and through perspiration, the body's efficient cooling mechanism. Some of that fluid is replaced by eating, as most of our food contains varying amounts of liquid; fresh fruits and vegetables contain relatively larger amounts, but even seemingly dry food like bread contains some liquid. In addition to the liquid in food, however, a daily intake of about two quarts of fluid is thought necessary to maintain proper body function.

Water—plain fresh water—is the simplest and most satisfactory way to provide our bodies with adequate fluids. Salt water is useless because it dehydrates body fluids more quickly than it replenishes them; who can forget the heartfelt lament of Coleridge's Ancient Mariner?

Water, water, everywhere,
Nor any drop to drink.

So fundamental is fresh water to human life that throughout our history it was one of the most important elements in how and where we chose to live; human settlement and migration were in large part dictated by the need for fresh drinkable water supplied by rivers, lakes, wells, and underground streams. Oases in the desert are legendary, but no less impressive are the varieties of human ingenuity in discovering and exploiting all kinds of resources that provided emergency rations of water in extreme climatic and geographic conditions. Native Americans sucked life-giving fluids from cactus plants that stored water in their fleshy parts, while the Bushmen of the Kalahari Desert traditionally used hollow reeds inserted in the earth to draw up precious water from below dried-up lake beds.

So for all of us, no matter who we are or where we live, water is crucial; it is a simple substance that is for the most part widely available and capable of fulfilling our fluid needs completely and satisfactorily without any alteration or transformation. From the point of view of its physiological function, plain water is the perfect liquid, and yet we humans have consistently chosen to change it, to refashion it, to take our fluids in forms that fulfill other needs and provide other satisfactions. Thirst, like hunger, is a basic drive that must be fulfilled in order for life to be sustained, but once that goal has been achieved, the uniquely human inclination for increased palatability, aesthetic gratification, and social expression comes into play, encouraging the transformation of simple water into more elaborate beverages. And these beverages, like our prepared food, take on attributes, values, and meaning that go well beyond their function of allaying thirst and providing our bodies with necessary fluids.

Whatever form these essential liquids may take, they are not all necessarily considered to be beverages. Whether a particular substance is eaten or drunk depends on the culture's view of it as a food or a beverage. Many people in a wide variety of cultures regard soup as food, even though it is frequently composed almost completely of liquid. Mexican cuisine has an interesting classification of some foods as *sopa seca*, or "dry soup," which refers to a pasta or grain cooked in a liquid that is eventually absorbed. Still, for most of us, soup means liquid—but a liquid food, not a drink. And conversely, while not all liquids are beverages, not all beverages are liquid. The prime example is the beverage that is the frequent alternative to the Coke on our cheeseburger platter.

The chocolate shake—thick, viscous, better eaten with a spoon than sucked through a straw—is a semisolid substance that is nonetheless considered to be a beverage, something to be drunk.

There are few cultures, if any, that do not fashion some kind of beverage, and most agree on the designation of substances as either food or drink (soup is food, beer is drink). The classification does not seem to be based on any obvious criteria; liquidity is not necessarily the defining characteristic, as we have seen, and the nutritive content also does not seem to be crucial. A clear consommé, with little body, no solid matter, and few calories is still regarded as soup, and therefore food, while a glass of milk, with its abundance of protein, fat, and carbohydrate, is considered to be a beverage. Once the milk is combined with other ingredients, however, and cooked into another substance like a sauce or a pudding, it becomes a food. So while most people may agree about what is food and what is drink, the criteria for those judgments are not at all clear.

All this needs to be taken note of because, in the course of fulfilling our fluid needs with beverages rather than pure simple water, we have produced some mighty strange substances—drinks that seem to go far beyond their primary function of satisfying thirst. In creating beverages, we change the sensory attributes of water—the color, the flavor, the aroma, the texture, and the temperature. We characteristically add nutrients, for remember that except for trace minerals, plain water contains no nutrients and no calories. And we frequently require our beverages to provide pharmacologic effects and deliberately fashion them to serve as medicines, stimulants, or intoxicants. All of these characteristics, found in our cup or can of icy Coke, are the very ones that all humans everywhere have sought in their beverages in the shift from plain water to elaborated drinks.

We don't know what the first created beverages were, but they are very likely to have been some kind of herbal teas or infusions, brewed for their medicinal properties. Our long-distant ancestors, as well as traditional cultures today, had extensive knowledge of plant life and developed many sophisticated traditions for using different plant parts for their pharmacologically active ingredients. The bark of the willow tree, boiled in water, has been used from ancient times to alleviate pain and bring down fever. It contains salicylic acid, a compound that is very similar chemically to acetylsalicylic acid, which we know as aspirin, still one of the most potent of pain- and fever-reducing agents. The perennial weed Saint-John's-wort was used to cure a variety of ailments; the sixteenth-century English herbalist Gerard wrote of this plant: "His flowers and seed boyled and drunken, provoketh urine, and is right good against stone in the bladder." North American people boiled the pulverized roots of the native sarsaparilla plant to make a tea that was drunk as a remedy for coughs; sarsaparilla, as well as its cousins birch beer and root beer, reemerged as sweetened soft drinks in the nineteenth and twentieth centuries. Hundreds of such liquid folk remedies were discovered and developed in cultures throughout the world. All of these decoctions, teas, and medicinal infusions made from roots, bark, seeds, flowers, and leaves changed simple water into beverages whose color, flavor, and physiologic effects were very striking—and this may well have set people on a deliberate experimental path of manipulating and refashioning their fluid intake.

While a cup of hot herbal tea might have relieved a cough or fever or provided a pleasant comforting warmth on a cold winter night, a glass of beer or wine offered consolations of quite another sort. Fermented beverages, made from a wide variety of grains and fruits, are another ancient human tradition whose origins are obscured in the dim mists of our early history. As we noted in our investigation of leavened bread, fermentation is a process that occurs naturally when wild yeasts, microorganisms ever-present in the natural environment, find a source of sugar on which to feed. In the course of digesting these sugars in a liquid medium, the yeasts produce carbon dioxide and alcohol, and a lightly carbonated, mildly alcoholic drink is the frequent result. These fermented liquids not only offered novel flavors and palate experiences but also provided a relaxing and pleasurable mild intoxication in a calorically rich fluid form.

Since yeasts feed on simple sugars, the earliest of these beverages was probably an accidental discovery, a drink made from the chance fermentation of overripe fruit or fruit with a high sugar content, like dates. Another possibility is honey, which was the only significant widespread sweet substance in the ancient world. Mead, the early drink of fermented honey and water, was widely known and appreciated, for both its alcoholic content and its sweetness. Later, when people began to collect or cultivate different fruits and vegetables, they used these to fashion a variety of sweet wines and ciders, reserving honey, which was a scarce and precious commodity, for exclusive use as a sweetener. And eventually, of course, the grape would emerge as the cultivated fruit of choice for fermenting into the most prestigious and valued of beverages, both in the ancient and contemporary worlds. The forerunners of our modern wines were frequently sweetened, with either honey or concentrated grape juice, to improve both their flavor and their storage life, and a variety of spices and other flavoring ingredients were sometimes added. From these simple sweet beginnings has evolved an enterprise of enormous variety and complexity, with hundreds of different wines offering a wide range of subtle flavors and bouquets and a wealth of sensory experiences.

The most common of fermented beverages is beer, also a drink of extreme antiquity. Although nowadays beer is brewed primarily from barley, it can be made from any number of grains, and it seems to have been discovered and enjoyed throughout the world wherever people had access to, or cultivated, the cereal grains. These beers might vary according to the climate, the location, and the type of grain, but the process and the product were much the same: wheat and barley beers in the Near and Middle East and Europe, millet beers in Africa and Central Asia, and in the Orient rice beers or, as they are more commonly known, rice wines. These rice brews are still rather than bubbly because they are fermented not with the yeasts that produce carbon dioxide, but with a kind of mold that grows on the rice grains. From ancient times in Central and South America a kind of beer was made from maize, the grain indigenous to the New World; in this case the fermentation process was initiated not by malting but by enzymes found in human saliva. The corn kernels were chewed and then allowed to ferment, and the resulting brew is still known as *chicha*.

The manufacture of beer is one step more complex than the making of mead or sweet fruit wines because the complex carbohydrates in the grains must be broken down into simpler sugars in order for fermentation to take place. Malting the grains initiates the process of fermentation, which then results in the characteristic production of alcohol and carbon dioxide.

Because malting changes starch to sugar, simple home-brewed beers were originally slightly sweet and probably somewhat flat in flavor. Produced in small batches for immediate consumption, they had no additional ingredients to lengthen their storage life. When the making of beer passed from the home kitchen to the commercial brewery, however, a variety of herbs and spices were added for preservative purposes, and these inevitably changed the flavor of the beer, shifting it from a sweet to a more bitter profile. In particular, the use of hops, an herb widely employed from medieval times to the present, provided commercial beers with their characteristic bitter flavor.

Beer is a term now used to describe a whole family of fermented grain beverages that exist in a dazzling variety of flavors, colors, and textures. Ale is made by the process of "top" fermentation, in which the yeast organisms do their work at the top of the fermenting brew; it is more perishable and generally richer and more complex in flavor than lager, which is made from a "bottom" fermentation. Lager is the type most characteristic of commercial American brews, with their clean, less pronounced flavor and longer storage life. Stouts and porters are historically more recent developments than beer, heavier, darker, "stouter" in body and flavor. All these fermented beverages that please so many with such a variety of forms began life as a homely, slightly sweet, and lightly carbonated drink, mildly alcoholic and rich in calories.

Of less antiquity than beer or wine, but certainly as widespread nowadays, are the hot stimulant beverages, coffee, tea, and chocolate. They originated in very different parts of the world—coffee in Africa, tea in China, chocolate in the tropics of Central America—and have very different histories, but they were all introduced into Europe at about the same time in the sixteenth century. They became the rage of that continent, and their use and preparation were remarkably similar despite their disparate origins. But all three were appreciated for much the same reason—their unique flavor and their refreshing stimulative properties.

Coffee is a beverage prepared from the roasted ground seeds of a tropical tree native to the mountains of Ethiopia and the Sudan. It contains caffeine, an alkaloid that acts as a stimulant on the nervous system, providing a refreshing sense of alertness. It is not at all clear that coffee was used as a beverage in its original homeland; rather, native Africans ground up the seeds and mixed them with fat into small balls. These concentrated and efficient little food packages provided a rich source of calories from the fat and a stimulating pick-me-up from the caffeine that could easily be carried on a long and tiring hunt. It was the Arab culture of North Africa that apparently developed the art of brewing ground coffee into a hot drink, thick, potent, and highly sweetened. Because alcoholic beverages were forbidden to the faithful of Islam, the double whammy of caffeine and sugar in a concentrated little cup provided a sanctioned pleasurable lift; when coffee was introduced by the Arabs into Europe, the Church of Rome denigrated it as the "wine of Islam." Although it was the

Arabs who first sweetened coffee, it was not until the beverage reached Europe that it was smoothed, diluted, and enriched with milk or cream.

Of apparently much greater antiquity than coffee is tea, a beverage made from the leaves of an evergreen bush native to Southeast Asia. A number of apocryphal stories recount the origin of this popular drink; one describes a Chinese emperor some four thousand years ago who was boiling water in his garden when by chance some leaves from a nearby bush fell into the pot. The emperor, a man of high taste and refinement, appreciated instantly the refreshing and stimulating qualities of this leafy brew, and so was discovered the drink that would become the standard beverage of Asia and which today is consumed on a daily basis by at least one half of the world's population. Tea contains caffeine, as well as a chemically related alkaloid, theophylline, and is highly aromatic and subtly flavorful. Introduced into Europe by Dutch and English navigators, it had its major impact on the English table, where it replaced home-brewed beer as the standard breakfast beverage. Its appearance in the West was coincident with the increasing availability of cane sugar, and while it had always been consumed unsweetened in its Asian homeland, it became highly sweetened in English tradition, where it remains the hot stimulant beverage of choice.

We don't know when chocolate was first discovered, but it was certainly an established tradition in Aztec culture by the time the Spanish arrived in Mexico in 1519. So valuable were cacao beans, imported from their native home in the tropics of Central America, that they were used as a form of currency. To make the ancient beverage *xocoatl* (the word is said to derive from the Nahuatl term for "bitter water"), fermented roasted cacao beans were ground into a thick paste, spiced with chile peppers, then whipped with water to make a thick foamy drink. The Aztecs considered chocolate to be a potent aphrodisiac, and the emperor Montezuma consumed many goblets of it daily, particularly before visiting his numerous wives. Chocolate contains caffeine, though in lesser amounts than coffee or tea, and another alkaloid, theobromine. The name of that compound, conferred by the Swedish naturalist Linnaeus in the eighteenth century, reflects chocolate's ancient and contemporary panache, for theobromine means "food of the gods." Chocolate is a mildly stimulant beverage but unlike coffee and tea also contains significant nutrients in the form of cocoa butter; ground cacao beans contain about fifty-five percent fat. No wonder, then, that the conquistador Cortés observed that "one cup of this precious drink permits a man to walk for a whole day without eating." Like the ground coffee-fat balls of African tradition, chocolate provided a concentrated source of energy and a stimulant in one easy mouthful, and although the bitter flavor of unsweetened chocolate was not much appreciated by Europeans, that was soon to be remedied. Chocolate joined coffee and tea on the tables of the well-to-do of Europe as a sweetened hot beverage, an energizing refreshment that enjoys to this day its delicious reputation as an aphrodisiac. It would not be until well into the nineteenth century, however, that chocolate would achieve its apotheosis as a luxurious and indulgent confection, a food rather than a beverage. And it was not until well into the twentieth that it would team up with milk, cream, and carbonated water to form an entirely new complex of sweetened cold beverages—the sodas, malteds, frosteds, and frappés that are so beloved a part of the American scene.

All of these, then—the herbal and medicinal teas; the hot stimulant beverages coffee, tea, and chocolate; the vast array of beers and wines; and juices pressed from fruits or cooked into syrups to mix with water—are the primary creations of the venerable human beverage tradition. And there were as well the potent distilled alcoholic spirits concocted from a huge assortment of ingredients, some as unlikely as cactus and potatoes, and flavored with everything from the juniper berries that gave gin its name to the Mexican caterpillar grub that gives mescal its special savor. Some know these beverages as whiskey or brandy or liqueur, others as firewater or moonshine or white lightning, names that are evocative of their very special qualities and their necessarily limited use.

All of these beverages are based, in one way or another, on water; all provide profound and unique experiences of flavor, color, texture, aroma, and physiological effect; and all play an important role in the expression of our social and ritual beliefs. We toast the bride and groom with champagne, not water; we invite a new neighbor over for a cup of coffee, not a glass of water; we celebrate our holidays with eggnog and spiced wine; and when we are sick we are comforted with steaming nurturant brews. Water is essential to life, but our beverages are essential to living, and we value them for all kinds of meaning that we have imbued them with. How, then, does the Coke and its associated soft drinks fit into or exemplify what it is that humans have consistently sought in refashioning water into more complex and attractive drinks?

What is fundamental and common to contemporary soft drinks—the colas, the fruit-flavored sodas, the root beers and the ginger ales—is that they are all sweet, they are all consumed cold, and they are all carbonated. Sweetness, as we noted earlier, is a taste that is immensely appealing to the American palate, and although Americans, like their English forebears, have thoroughly exploited and indulged their passion for sugar, they are not alone in finding the taste attractive and desirable. The taste for sweetness seems to be universal in our species and we apparently come into the world already programmed to respond positively to it. This may be because the very first food we consume, mother's milk, is sweet in flavor (and among other mammalian milks, human milk is unusually sweet). Or it may be that sweetness points to a quick and easy source of energy. In any case, as humans we all seem to like it, although we all deal with it differently in our culinary traditions. Mediterranean cuisines, as well as the French, use sugar much less frequently as a flavoring ingredient in savory cooked food than do Southeast Asian cuisines, for example; the Chinese are masters at using sweetness to enhance complex flavoring systems. A less heavy use of sugar and sweetness seems to correlate with a strong wine-drinking tradition, but it probably corresponds ultimately with much broader issues of geography, resources, and availability of ingredients.

So while culinary traditions vary significantly as to how they use and value sugar and sweetness, most seem to enjoy it as an important part of the beverage experience. Whether the sweetness occurs naturally, as in fruit juices or simple beers and wines, or whether the sweetness is added, as it is to sweetened wines, coffee, tea, chocolate, and soft drinks, sweet liquids have a strong universal appeal. Not only is the taste attractive but the physiological effect is also clear and immediate—a powerful jolt of energy rapidly delivered to the bloodstream (unless, of course, you are drinking a diet beverage, in which case you get the pleasant sweet taste without the calories). Indeed, sucrose dissolved in water is the simplest and most efficient form of energy, an extremely palatable source of quick nourishment.

What may further account for the strong appeal of sweet beverages, particularly in the Western world, is that in its early history sugar was widely regarded as a medicinal substance. This was no doubt due in part to the fact that it was rare and costly; it was thought to alleviate the symptoms of many ailments, to coat the throat, and to soothe the digestive system. In its most refined form as a pure white crystal it was believed to have many special curative powers, and as late as the eighteenth century in England was prescribed, along with other precious ingredients, as a remedy for a variety of ills. The tradition of sweetened liquids as medicines continues today with tea and honey, sweet cough syrups, and hot toddies; in these preparations the sweetness is considered to be beneficial as well as pleasant. There is something deep in our traditional practice that sees sweet liquids as not only good-tasting but good for us.

The issue of temperature in our soft drink is more complex, for until fairly recently most people did not have access to the refrigerators and freezers on which we modern folk so depend; we take for granted our refrigerated drinks, their chill further enhanced with shaved ice or ice cubes. Is this insistence on super coldness simply a fluke of the contemporary scene, an inevitable result of modern technology, or is there something else involved? Actually, when one looks at the whole human beverage tradition, it becomes clear that people seem historically to have preferred their drinks either hot or cold, but not tepid or lukewarm, and the reasons for this preference lie deep in the collective unconscious. We must have water to live, yet water is a substance extremely vulnerable to microbial infestation. Warm or tepid water is an ideal breeding medium for all sorts of bacteria, viruses, parasites, and other microorganisms that can cause infection, debilitating illness, even death; humans must surely have learned very early in their history how dangerous water could be. In fact, it is likely that concern for health and safety, rather than sensory or aesthetic issues, initially motivated people to manipulate their fluids, in an attempt to provide safe and healthful drinks from possibly contaminated water.

Boiling water is one of the easiest and most obvious ways to kill offending microorganisms, and this may be the reason that drinks made from hot water were our first "safe" beverages. In addition, many herbs and plant substances must be steeped or brewed in boiling water in order for their aromatic and medicinal properties to be released. Remember the story of the origin of tea: The emperor was boiling water when some leaves happened to fall into the pot. The emperor was boiling water because the Chinese were, from ancient times, extraordinarily sophisticated and knowledgeable about health and medicine, and understood the benefits of boiled water and the possible dangers of untreated water.

So it may be that we find hot beverages attractive because they represent safety while providing a heartwarming, comforting, and healing drink. But what about cold drinks? For after all, chilling water does not necessarily kill offending organisms the way boiling does. Still, cold water is less likely to harbor dangerous substances than warm or tepid water; most of us would far sooner drink the water from a cold rushing stream than from a still warm pond, and we would be justified in making that choice. Cold water, particularly moving cold water, provides some assurance of clarity and purity, and cold liquids further enhance our perception of being refreshed, of having our thirst quenched. This may be because cold drinks can be consumed more quickly than hot drinks, and the momentary chilling of the mouth gives an overall sensation of refreshing coolness. There are, however, no absolute criteria for what temperatures provide the optimum experience. For most of history people enjoyed beers, wines, and ciders cooled in underground caves or cellars, while we contemporary consumers seem to require far more frigid drinks. This preference may reveal the constant and widespread human desire to up the sensory ante. If cold is good, then icy is better.

If the sensory gratification that we seek in our beverages is provided by their flavor and temperature, it seems to be further enhanced by carbonation—that is, the saturation of water with bubbles of carbon dioxide. Our modern sodas, as well as many sparkling wines and beers, are artificially carbonated, but carbonation is a process that occurs naturally, given certain conditions of heat and pressure. Ancient people, at least in some parts of the world, must have encountered naturally carbonated waters in underground mineral springs and pools. These waters, with their tingly effervescence, have long been considered beneficial to bathe or soak in—and if they were good for our outsides, then why not for our insides? And carbonation occurs naturally as well, as we have seen, in the course of fermentation, producing fizzy liquids like beer, hard cider, and sparkling wine. So it seems we have a long acquaintance with and great affection for bubbles in our brew.

The question is, why do we like them so much? First of all, there is a long and widely held belief that carbonated beverages are good for us, having the capacity to aid the digestion and settle the stomach. This may be due to the fact that swallowing bubbles of gas helps to dislodge gas already present in the stomach, thus affording some temporary relief. And because carbon dioxide does in fact have some antibacterial properties, carbonated liquids are likely to be somewhat safer and healthier than noncarbonated liquids. In addition, recent research has shown that carbonation heightens our perception of coldness in liquids, and since coldness is already a desirable attribute, an intensification of the sensation is positive. Carbonation provides movement as well, reinforcing the perception of pure, clean, running water. Last, and I think most important, is that bubbles, fizz, and effervescence provide the mouth with an extraordinary and unprecedented stimulation.

The interesting fact is that we don't experience carbonation as bubbles, but rather as tingly little pinpricks, sharp little bursts on the mouth and palate. The sensations we feel are akin to, but not quite, pain, an irritant stinging that is intensified by colder temperatures. In this sense, the action of carbonation in liquids is very similar to that of chile peppers in food, producing a slightly painful but pleasurable sensation that lights up the mouth, heightening and intensifying the other palate experiences of flavor, temperature, and texture or body. The whole act of consumption is made fuller, richer, more exciting; the tiny bubbles that sting our palate and fly up our nose make us actively aware that we have drunk and that we have been refreshed. What chile peppers do for boring food, carbonation does for boring liquids, acting as a kind of super-stimulus for the experience of drinking.

If a pleasant sweet taste and a refreshing effervescence were enough to make our cold beverages completely satisfying, then we might all have remained content with the myriad fruit-flavored sodas that developed in the middle of the nineteenth century and that have become standards in the soft drink industry. But the hands-down worldwide favorite is a relative latecomer, the Coke, invented in the last decades of the nineteenth century by an Atlanta pharmacist who was seeking not a recipe for a pleasant soft drink but a remedy for headaches and dyspepsia. And *that* may well be the key to the ultimate success of Coke and the subsequent raft of imitative colas. For as our brief review of the long human beverage tradition has indicated, we clearly like, and consequently design, our drinks to provide us with some kind of pharmacological effect. The medicinal properties of herbal teas, the intoxicant effects of alcoholic beverages, the stimulant qualities of coffee, tea, and chocolate all point to a very widespread tendency to use beverages for mood alteration, to make ourselves feel good while we quench our thirst and please our taste buds.

The original formula for Coke, which remains to this day a closely guarded secret, is said to have included extracts from both coca leaves—the very same used in the manufacture of cocaine—and kola nuts, which African natives have long chewed for their stimulant effects. Hence the name Coca-Cola. The coca leaves were quickly abandoned, but kola nuts, as well as caffeine, are still used to give Coke and other colas their refreshing stimulant properties. A "typical" cola beverage contains the following ingredients: water, sugar, phosphoric acid, caffeine, carbon dioxide, gum acacia, caramel color, nutmeg oil, orange oil, lemon oil, vanilla, lime oil, cinnamon oil, kola nut extract, cassia oil, and clove oil. The resulting flavor is complex—sweet, fruity, spicy, and somewhat medicinal, with a rich brown "brewed" color and a substantial body, provided primarily by the sugar. The acid adds tartness, modifies the sweetness, and enhances the thirst-quenching effects by stimulating saliva. The caffeine, used in much smaller amounts than are found in a cup of coffee, provides a pleasant lift but not enough to violate our notions of what is appropriate stimulation for children, who are traditionally denied the other common stimulant and intoxicant beverages. All in all, it is a supremely successful formula and one that has found favor well beyond its original American homeland.

It should come as no surprise, then, that the Coke is the beverage of choice on the cheeseburger platter, but here, in addition to the positive characteristics for which it is esteemed, it has some other rather more subtle functions to perform. The meal we love so much contains a substantial load of fat, which coats the mouth and tongue; after a couple of bites, this fat becomes unappetizing and dulls the appetite. Coke seems to be very effective at cleansing and refreshing the palate, first because of its spicy medicinal flavor and second because of its heavy carbonation; "medicinal" soft drinks like the colas, root beer, and ginger ale are traditionally more heavily carbonated than fruit-flavored sodas. Whether that cleansing is real or simply perceived is not clear; plain water or a hot beverage might do the job as well or better, but Coke provides the critical perception of ultra-refreshment. It is not an unlikely function; the French would surely grimace with distaste at the notion of cleansing the palate with Coke, but they traditionally use very similar substances, icy sweet-tart fruit sorbets, to provide refreshment between courses.

All cultures have beverages that are traditional favorites; some of these are nearly universal, while others are more culturally individualistic. The thick, sweet coconut or avocado drinks of Malaysia, the salty yogurt beverages of Iran, the whipped sweet fruity yogurt *lassis* of India, the fermented mare's milk of Central Asia, the yak-butter tea of Tibet are all entrenched traditional favorites whose appeal is limited to the cultural milieu from which they emerged. But King Coke, along with its cohorts of sweet, cold, carbonated drinks, all pleasant, reliable, familiar, and cheap, has transcended national and cultural barriers, providing a beverage that appeals to almost every taste. While refreshment, hospitality, and the social exchange can be expressed or achieved in any number of ways, Coke is unique as a universally accepted beverage, no small accomplishment for a drink that began life only one hundred years ago as a quick fix for an upset tummy. Slick packaging and clever marketing aside, the Coke has much that we have wanted from our beverages throughout our history, a sweet, safe, refreshing lift in one deliciously easy gulp.

Eight

THE LAND OF THE FREE
AND THE HOME OF
THE BURGER

*H*aving chomped our way through the meal that provides such deep gratification for so many of us, it is perhaps time to lick a greasy finger or two, indulge in a satisfying reflective burp, and sit back to consider how this unique and surprising assemblage of foods arose from its particular cultural and historic milieu as a characteristic culinary expression of the American experience. In our search for the significance of its seemingly near universal appeal, we have implicated the tastes and the traditions of our earliest ancestors, as well as the practices and preferences of a wide variety of cuisines throughout history and across the world. But the cheeseburger platter is wholeheartedly and uncontestedly American, a fact made no less true by its popularity in Paris, Rio, and Beijing.

The cheeseburger was not designed; it did not spring full-blown from the head of some mad advertising genius bent on forcing his twisted culinary vision on an innocent and unsuspecting world. Like any other cultural form it evolved, slowly

at first, as we have seen, over long undocumented generations, then, at the end, very quickly, as the appropriate ingredients and forces coalesced in the American homeland to
create its unique character. And it is still evolving, for cuisine
is rarely static, particularly in an environment as dynamic and
as multiethnic as America. With the sprout-and-tofu burger
and the seaweed burger already under our belt, can the quinoa
burger or the goat-cheese-and-walnut burger be far behind?

The name itself is a clue to its complex and muddy origins,
for while *burger* is now a thoroughly American term—as
American, indeed, as apple pie (which is really English, but
who's quibbling?)—it is clearly a name of German derivation,
an affectionate shortening of the original *hamburger*. *Hamburger* has nothing to do with ham, of course, but comes from
the name for the first widely acknowledged ground beef patty
consumed in America. This was the "Hamburg steak," an
oval cake of ground or finely minced lean beef, pan-fried in
butter and served with fried onions and frequently a gravy
made from the pan drippings. It is what is more commonly
known today as "Salisbury steak," and it remains an old-
fashioned American favorite. It is not entirely clear why the
Hamburg steak was so named, but the prevailing view is that
the dish originated in the city of Hamburg, a port situated
on the Baltic Sea, which had, in the fifth century A.D., been
in contact with invading tribes from Central Asia. These war-
like nomads, whom we first encountered in Chapter 1, are

credited with the invention of steak tartare, that unique dish of flavored minced raw meat, and are thought to have passed the tradition on to Western Europe through eastern Germany and the Baltic connection. Except for the grinding of the meat, however, evidence of a relationship between steak tartare and the Hamburg steak is not overwhelming; steak tartare remains what it has always been—a raw meat preparation—while the other is a cooked and sauced dish, known in Hamburg, incidentally, as a "German beefsteak." In fact, the designation "German" may well be a way of distinguishing a traditional cooked ground meat patty from the more exotic raw Asian preparation. And there is little reason to suppose that Europe learned about mincing meat from these foreign invaders of the Asian steppes; there was, after all, a long-established tradition of loaves, pâtés, rissoles, wursts, and sausages, all of which involved the chopping or grinding, seasoning, and cooking of meat.

The fried sauced ground beef patty was perceived in America as German in origin, if for no other reason than that it was a food commonly eaten by German immigrants, and it remained known as the Hamburg steak until the time it was placed, with its accompanying fried onions but minus the gravy, between two slices of bread. With this innovation it was transformed from a plated entrée into a handheld sandwich, to be known henceforth as the Hamburger, while *hamburger* was to become a widely used synonym for the raw material from which hamburgers are made. (A nonnative speaker might well be puzzled by the utterance: "I'm going to the store to buy some hamburger for the hamburgers.") The credit for the invention of the hamburger sandwich, clearly a landmark event, is in dispute; some attribute it to a nameless German factory owner who, at the turn of the century, devised it as a quick, efficient, and filling hot lunch for his workers. A prior origin is claimed by the town of Seymour, Wisconsin, where, at the Outagamie County Fair in October 1885, a gentleman named Charles R. Nagreen—subsequently dubbed Hamburger Charlie—flattened his fried meatballs, slapped them between two slices of bread, and sold them as portable meals to fairgoers. Seymour celebrates itself as the "home of the hamburger" with such annual events as the cooking of a 5,520-pound hamburger and the International Hamburger Olympics, featuring the "ketchup slide." What is not in dispute is the first introduction of the burger on a grander national scale; in 1904 at the International Exposition in St. Louis the hamburger appeared along with such sterling innovations as ground peanut butter and the ice-cream cone.

From this point the burger became instantly popular as the ideal exemplar of the savory hot handheld meal, serving both as a quick lunch for office and factory workers and as an attractive and filling snack at ballparks, fairgrounds, and zoos. It appeared regularly as well on the menus of diners, luncheonettes, and popular restaurants, and became, along with the beef stew, the pot roast, and the meatloaf, a traditional preparation of the home kitchen and the backyard barbecue. The burger was not, in other words, a rare and exotic new dish, but rather an agreeable new arrangement of already familiar foods presented in a novel and accessible form, one that seized the popular imagination and the mainstream palate. Whatever the specifics of its very first incarnation, it was clearly something that was ready to happen, and when it did, it did so in a great popular explosion that propelled it into every corner of the land. Whether at home or in a variety of public places, the burger was from the start widely available, cheap, easy to prepare, and even easier to consume. In the 1920s White Castle opened the first burger chain; a sack of twenty burgers could be had for one dollar. Burger emporia burgeoned throughout the landscape, and in the forties and fifties, when all America was on wheels, the drive-through chains emerged, with McDonald's and Big Boy and Burger King delivering what was by this time an entrenched and well-loved meal through the window of one's car. By now the cheese, the fries, and the Coke had joined ranks with the classic burger, and the appeal of this efficient and delicious meal was apparently irresistible.

With the proliferation of the burger as a classic form came the inevitable development of variations on the theme—burgers composed of ingredients other than beef and garnished with a variety of different foods. What remained constant was a fried or grilled patty made of meat or of some ground or particulated substance that approximated the texture of ground meat. For vegetarians were created the nut burger, the falafel burger (made of ground spiced chickpeas or fava beans), and the soy burger (composed of soybeans processed to look and feel like meat). For pork lovers came sausage burgers and Spam burgers, though never, curiously, a real *ham* burger. And for connoisseurs of ethnic diversity there developed such varieties as the Aloha burger, seasoned with soy sauce and garnished with a pineapple ring; the California burger, topped with alfalfa sprouts and sliced avocado; the pizza burger, topped with spaghetti sauce and melted mozzarella; the Tex-Mex burger, garnished with spicy salsa and jack cheese; and the chili burger, doused with a messy spoonful of beef and/or bean chili, shredded cheese, lettuce, and chopped tomato.

While the burger flowered into a number of diverse forms, constrained only by regional preference and the cook's imagination, the issue of size has almost never been questioned. If big was good, then bigger was better; the simple single burger, with its accompanying layers of cheese, ketchup, onions, and pickles, soon divided like a giant amoeba and expanded into double and then triple layers. The burger franchises competed on the basis of size, with the Big Mac, the Big Boy, and the Whopper, like a trio of street bullies, all asserting their claim as the *biggest*—and therefore the best. (It is perhaps worth noting here that the burger is decidedly male in character and is consistently paraded and described in traditionally macho terms.) Individual entrepreneurs jumped on the bandwagon with such megaburgers as the Belly Bomber, the Belly Buster, and the Giganta-burger. Only once did the commercial burger tradition flirt with the reverse notion of a dainty miniburger; in the early 1990s, when diet and health issues were becoming a national obsession, some franchises introduced miniature hamburgers, cute as all get-out—and clearly unacceptable to burger-eating Americans. When it comes to our favorite meal, the health risks be damned! We want it big, with all its sensory attributes intact and in plenty, a large juicy satisfying handful, not a mincing little morsel to be popped delicately into the mouth. (As this book went to press, in the winter of 1994, Burger King proudly introduced its Mega Double Cheese, a "colossal," "gargantuan," "behemoth" of a burger. So much for mini!)

In little more than a hundred years the burger has evolved from its rather mundane beginnings as a sauced knife-and-fork entrée to the extravagantly garnished meal-on-a-bun that is the hallmark of popular American taste. It is to be had in every corner of the country, from remote country inns to roadside diners to upscale city bistros. Indeed, as Charles Kuralt, that wise and witty commentator on the American scene, has observed: "You can find your way across this country using burger joints the way a navigator uses stars. . . . We have munched Bridge burgers in the shadow of Brooklyn Bridge and Cable burgers hard by the Golden Gate, Dixie burgers in the sunny South and Yankee Doodle burgers in the North. . . . We had a Capitol burger—guess where. And so help us, in the inner courtyard of the Pentagon, a Penta burger."

How did this amazing phenomenon come about? If all that we have speculated about in the preceding chapters has any validity, if indeed the cheeseburger meal represents some kind of ideal realization of so much that all humans have sought from their food experience, then why did it take so long to achieve, and why did it take shape so quickly when it finally did?

The reasons are many and complex, of course, but absolutely fundamental to the development of the cheeseburger was the European discovery and acquisition of the New World, initiated by Columbus's landing in the Bahamas in October 1492. The opening of the Americas uncovered a wealth of land and resources that was infinitely more valuable than the gold and spices of the Orient that European navigators had sought; here for the taking were vast ranges and grasslands on which to raise, on an unprecedented scale, the domesticated cattle that would provide the beef for which Europeans lusted. Here were unlimited fertile prairies, with their rich virginal soil, to grow wheat for the settlers' bread, and corn and soybeans to feed their livestock. Here were the rich southern delta lands and the subtropical islands where sugar cane could flourish on a scale grand enough to assuage the aching sweet tooth of the new Americans. From the purely geographic perspective this New World provided in abundance the rich lands and resources necessary to cultivate the crops and the animals for which emigrating Europeans already had a taste, and it supplied as well the two indigenous foods that would ultimately complete the cheeseburger meal —the tomatoes for the ketchup and the potatoes for the french fries.

Also critical to the emergence of the cheeseburger platter were increasing urbanization, mechanization, and industrialization. In the nineteenth century, as people swelled the growing cities of America, a number of developments in technology permitted them access to many foods that had been previously unavailable or that were produced solely for home consumption on family farms. Pasteurization, canning, and bottling were all newly developed techniques that allowed the widespread distribution of processed food products; cowboys herding cattle on Texas ranges quenched their thirst with tomatoes canned on the East Coast, while New Yorkers dined on cheese manufactured in Chicago and ketchup and pickles produced in Pittsburgh. The techniques for carbonating and bottling flavored soft drinks were perfected, and bottled "pop" took off as the nation's choice of a safe, attractive, and widely acceptable beverage. And as the end of the Civil War united the North and the South, politically if not emotionally, the transcontinental railroad made its ultimate hookup in the middle of the century, finally and irrevocably joining the East to the West, the Atlantic to the Pacific—and America was one. Now the great herds of western cattle made their way to the stockyards and meat packers of the Midwest, where they were slaughtered, processed, and shipped across the country in a great tidal wave of beef.

With all these changes in transportation and technology came a major shift in lifestyle from the rural to the urban, with people much less dependent on the home kitchen as the source of all meals. With so many working outside the home, a new way of eating evolved to meet the needs of those who were ever more constrained by a time clock and an ever-watchful boss. We were a people on the move—busy, energetic, ambitious—and the quick, efficient, yet satisfying meal became an essential feature of many lives for at least one meal of the day. The sandwich in general and the hot nourishing hamburger in particular provided a perfect solution to the need to eat on the run, to be gratified with attractive belly-filling food while wasting not a minute of that ever more precious commodity, time. And wherever we traveled, from home to the job, from the country to the city, from the city to the suburbs, across this vast country with its ethnic diversity and regional individuality, the burger emerged as the standard of the All-American food, recognizable, familiar, and acceptable to all.

But while land and resources, technology and changing lifestyles were all essential factors, it was above all the national character itself that would lead to the distinctive nature of the nation's favorite food. The American character is as diverse and contradictory as the people who make it up, a unique and unprecedented mélange of races, religions, ethnicities, and politics. It is a character in some ways utterly fragmented but united in one crucial respect—that it created itself as it created this new country, a country where there was no past (or at least no past that its new inhabitants chose to acknowledge or honor), a country where the future was all, where youth and vigor and toughness were what determined how or whether one prospered or declined. The accidents of birth or social standing, wealth or privilege, were no longer the sole determinants of a person's destiny, for here in this brawling and unparalleled new place where—theoretically, at any rate—everyone was equal, it was the individual who made his own life, by dint of hard work, dedication, endurance, and a not infrequent skulduggery. Here, as never anywhere else before, Everyman was king, and as he labored to build a better life and create a nation, he felt entitled as never before to the fruits of his labor and the rewards of hard work. Whatever those rewards might be—a new car or a new tractor, an education for the kids, a hot tub, or a nice hunk of beef—he felt he had earned them and that it was his right to enjoy them as amply as possible. The cheeseburger meal was for many a tangible, edible embodiment of the American dream.

As the American population grew more and more ethnically diverse, a number of parallel products evolved, food preparations that contained most of the salient components of the cheeseburger but in more ethnically delineated forms. However they may differ in detail, they are all structurally equivalent; like the cheeseburger they consist of two pieces of bread that enclose ground or finely sliced meat, with a savory sauce or condiment, some chopped or shredded vegetable, and a topping of melted cheese. Their sameness testifies to a profound and widespread taste for such products, sandwiches that are hot, handheld, layered meals in which all the components are experienced in a single mouthful. And like the cheeseburger they developed here, as American interpretations of other ethnic traditions.

Although most of these alternatives developed fairly late, in the second half of the twentieth century, the first of them made its appearance at about the same time as the hamburger. This was the hot dog, another food of German origin, a finely textured spiced pork and beef sausage served on an elongated bun and garnished with mustard and sauerkraut. Like the Hamburg steak, the frankfurter was originally a knife-and-fork food named for the city in Germany from which it was supposed to have come; for most Americans, not oversensitive to the subtleties of European geography, the frankfurter, or sausage from Frankfurt, would become synonymous with the wiener, or sausage from Vienna. But the minute the sausage was placed in a bun and hawked at ballparks around the turn of the century, it became thoroughly American; renamed the "hot dog," it evoked its German roots by its comic physical similarity to the popular dachshund. The hot dog has proved to be an enduring favorite, entering into the national argot both as an exclamation of pleasure or approval—"Hot DAWG!"—and as a term to describe overachieving showoffs who demand center stage. Like the hamburger, the hot dog has yielded variations such as the cheese dog, the chili dog, and the corn dog, but for all its enduring vitality here on its native shores, it never achieved the great success abroad that the cheeseburger so easily attained; the flavored, spiced sausage meat, the mustard, and the kraut make it far less acceptable to a variety of other culinary traditions.

While the hot dog kept its basic German identity as it insinuated itself into the American experience, a number of other ethnic sandwich varieties developed that reflect the growing diversification of the population and an expanding sophistication of the national palate, a willingness to try the special foods and flavors of other groups. From the exploding passion for Italian food has emerged the meatball hoagie, known also in different regions as a submarine sandwich, grinder, or hero. This sloppy delight consists of cooked spiced meatballs nestled in a long Italian roll, topped with savory tomato sauce, onions and peppers, and melted mozzarella cheese. A specialty of Philadelphia is the cheese steak, an Italian roll filled with finely shaved grilled beef, topped with sautéed onions and melted cheese, and garnished, at the diner's discretion, with either tomato sauce or ketchup. The Mexican version of the meal-in-the-hand, which came to the mainstream via the Tex-Mex cuisines of the Southwest, is the taco, a corn tortilla fried and folded to enclose spicy ground beef in tomato sauce, topped with salsa, lettuce, and shredded cheese. And the "deli" version, a product of urban America with its large populations of assimilated Jews who no longer observe the strict dietary laws regarding the mixing of meat and dairy products, is the Reuben, a sandwich of grilled rye bread filled with finely sliced corned beef or pastrami, garnished with sauerkraut, Thousand Island dressing, and melted Swiss cheese. Recently a vegetarian Reuben has appeared on the scene that substitutes grilled vegetables like eggplant, peppers, and mushrooms for the traditional spiced cured meats; it reflects a growing avoidance of meat, together with a strong reluctance to give up the savory sandwich.

Despite their clear structural similarities, these sandwiches are all very different from one another when viewed from an individual sensory and cultural perspective, even though their ethnicity has been substantially moderated, toned down,

"Americanized." While they are all widely appreciated in this country, their more specific ethnic character makes them less appealing in other parts of the world. In this category of foods the cheeseburger remains undisputed king, or rather elected head of state or speaker of the House, the common denominator of the form on which almost all can agree. It remains the most successful expression yet of the so-called melting pot, a genuine coming together of many of the world's traditions into something new and innovative, but shorn of ethnic or cultural specificity, a rendering in food of everything America has chosen to be.

Yet like so much that is unique to the American experience, this vital, successful, and enjoyable meal is not without its costs, costs that we can only begin to assess, and that may ultimately prove to be too high for the gratification provided. The price in human life is unimaginable, whole populations enslaved, degraded, and destroyed for the sake of an erupting European-based American appetite. The iniquitous institution of black slavery was initiated by the establishment of sugar cane plantations in the Caribbean manned by slaves from Africa; that profitable pandering to the American sweet tooth started something that will haunt this country, and the world, into the unforeseeable future. The indigenous cultures of the Great Plains were effectively wiped out, victims of the single-minded American dedication to acquisition and dominance; these native people, who had lived in harmony with the natural world for untold generations, were pushed aside and destroyed in the name of American advancement, their traditional food source, the wild buffalo, eradicated to make way for the cattle and the wheat demanded to satisfy America's taste for beef and white bread.

In ecological terms the cheeseburger's effect on the health of the planet is no more auspicious. Beef cattle are the most expensive and destructive of domesticated animals; in the heedless rush to gratify our long-evolving appetite for beef and to supply as cheaply as possible the central ingredient of burger franchises throughout the world, huge areas of natural habitat, including the invaluable and irreplaceable rain forests, are daily being destroyed to provide grazing land for more and more cattle. While that destruction of the earth's resources has, and will continue to have, clear and as yet unmeasurable effects across the globe, the methane gas produced by the ever-growing numbers of cattle is already apparently contributing to a deterioration in the earth's atmosphere. And while it is not within the domain of this book to assess the fast-food enterprise as a whole, the impact on the planet of a seemingly unlimited detritus of paper, plastic, and Styrofoam can hardly be ignored.

From the nutritional point of view the liabilities of the cheeseburger platter, particularly as presented by the fast-food franchises, have become alarmingly evident. The meal is caloric overkill, not necessarily a bad thing in and of itself, but certainly undesirable and perhaps even dangerous for people who are already overnourished. For many Americans and Europeans, long accustomed to a diet high in animal foods and fat, the cheeseburger is an agreeable and familiar assemblage of ingredients, but where once such a heavy and frequent dose of fat might not have exacted so large a toll, our overindulgence and our lack of physical activity result in the widespread medical problems of obesity and cardiac dysfunction. Similarly, the meal's exploitation of both salt and sugar to provide flavor is also medically suspect. Salt is a necessary mineral, but when overused can be implicated in a number of diseases, including hypertension. And sugar, or sucrose, historically a scarce and precious commodity, is linked in its contemporary abundance to diabetes, tooth decay, and hyperactivity. In its pleasurable and widely available form as a soft drink it frequently substitutes for other foods as a quick meal in itself, replacing other more valuable but perhaps less enticing nutrients; this may be a problem of particular relevance to young people and to third world people who have limited resources and little information about the relative values of different foods and who are particularly vulnerable to seductive sweetness.

From the gastronomic perspective the cheeseburger platter offends precisely for the same reasons that it succeeds, by catering to the lowest common denominator of human taste. It relies for its effect on all the super-stimuli that people have consistently found pleasant and rewarding throughout their eating history—fat, sweetness, "cheap" flavor, carbonation—in an abundant and easy form. Its direct and undisguised appeal to the lowest popular level is predicated on an almost complete absence of subtlety, nuance, refinement, or ethnic specificity. And because of the easiness and availability of fast food, we are raising generations of children both here and abroad whose gastronomic acumen is defined by—and limited to—Big Macs and Whoppers, with occasional diversions provided by Pizza Hut and Colonel Sanders. For palates nurtured on this agreeable but unchallenging sort of food, the complex dimensions of other kinds of eating become, unfortunately, largely inaccessible; a palate accustomed to the instant overwhelming pleasure of a Coke or a Pepsi or an Orange Crush is unlikely to respond positively to the subtleties of an aromatic unsweetened Darjeeling tea or a heady old burgundy, or even to a glass of pure fresh spring water. The point is not so much that we all need to be epicures, but that in a time and a place where so much is available to so many of us, one of the great social and aesthetic experiences of life is regrettably diluted, homogenized, and subverted.

Still, it is just a little patronizing, is it not, for us to disdain this ample and pleasing food as "junk" food? It is all well and good for those of us who care—and who have the means—to select our food and to shape our eating experiences with a fastidious regard to all the nutritional and aesthetic criteria that are currently fashionable. But we have, after all, the luxury of choice, something our species has not so frequently enjoyed in its food history. The cheeseburger meal may indeed be for many of us common, vulgar, unabashed in the directness of its low-level appeal, but from the broader perspective it offers much that is positive and valuable and that cannot be so easily dismissed.

Whatever the cheeseburger's fate may be, however it may ultimately be evaluated and experienced, it is an uncannily accurate culinary reflection of the land and the culture from which it arose. Here is a meal that developed out of the immigrant hodgepodge of North America and yet contains not a single food native to this continent. It has the beef and the cheese from Europe, the leavened wheat bread from the Middle East, ketchup from Southeast Asia, tomatoes from Mexico, sugar from India, kola nuts from Africa, potatoes from Peru, onions and pickles from just about everywhere. Foods from every corner of the globe, the tastes and traditions of all the world's people, come together on these shores to form an entirely new way to be and an entirely new way to eat.

And yet, for all its newness, it is not so new at all. For although the cheeseburger, with its layers and garnishes, its accompanying french fries and soft drink, is distinctly novel in its construction and presentation, it is at the same time recognizable, familiar, known. All the components are traditional and well liked by many people in different cultures; even the foods, like the tomatoes and the potatoes, that are in historical terms fairly recent to traditions outside the New World are prepared in ways that make them widely accessible and appealing. And it is precisely this resolution of the tension between the novel and the familiar that accounts for so much of the cheeseburger's success. For while it addresses itself to a common human experience, one that transcends the specifics of culture, time, and geography, it does so by constructing the experience in an interesting and exciting new way. The cheeseburger platter is on the one hand a novel and delightful meal, innovative, contemporary, fun; on the other hand it has much that is ancient and deep in the human experience, traditional and long familiar. We recognize it as our ancestors might have recognized it—as a modern variation on a set of old, old themes. Street food, fast food, is not, after all, a modern invention; it has existed as long as people have congregated in public places for commercial, ceremonial, or social purposes. And the taste for meat, for fat, for sweetness and salt, is as old as we are, satisfactions that are rediscovered with each new generation.

While the cheeseburger's appeal is clearly based on its satisfactory interpretation of so much that is common or universal in the human food tradition, its success rests equally on the promise and the delivery of abundance and fulfillment. This meal not only plays to ancient and widespread desires and preferences, but it does so with a generosity unprecedented in most human experience. So much that we have always craved, searched for, delighted in, is here, all together, in one gratifying luxurious meal. The meat and the fat, the sugar, the salt, the cold refreshing mouth-popping beverage are presented to us not isolated as small solitary indulgences, but in one grand extravagant whole. The vegetables, the grains, the savory condiments are here not as second-best substitutes for the meat and the fat we so love, but as pleasing extras that add complexities of texture and flavor, complementing the super-foods and the super-sensations that are central and crucial.

Despite its seeming simplicity, the cheeseburger platter is a megameal, one that thumbs its nose at the "thrifty" gene, the ability developed by so many of our ancestors through long, hard generations to get by on the scarcest of resources and the sparsest of nutrients, to survive and to prosper in the face of limited and sometimes unsatisfactory food. It is not at all surprising that the cheeseburger should have evolved in a time and a place where simply "getting by" was not good enough, where success is measured by consumption, not conservation. Our food reflects who we are and what we believe; it is simply food and has no moral or social or aesthetic value beyond that with which we invest it. If it offends or disappoints, the fault, dear reader, lies not in the food but in ourselves.

Whatever its costs, whatever its deficiencies, this American classic has answered a challenge and fulfilled a promise: a meal of plenty from this land of plenty, with something for everyone, and no one excluded from the feast. Not a bad legacy for the cheeseburger; not a bad mandate for America.

NOTES

CHAPTER ONE

10. "Consider, for example, the astonishingly wide range of taboos . . ." The subject of animal food avoidance is extensive and complex and can be approached and interpreted from any number of points of view—ecological, nutritional, ritual, symbolic. The most comprehensive and thorough review is to be found in *Eat Not This Flesh* by the economic geographer Frederick J. Simoons.

18. "Our finicky Western sensibilities . . ." A fascinating study—along with recipes—of animal foods and animal parts rejected as unfit or unappealing by American tradition is presented in *Unmentionable Cuisine* by Calvin W. Schwabe.

26. "Imagine it thus . . ." I have elected to make the discoverer of cooked meat a female because the evidence seems to indicate that women are more sensitive to and discrimi-

natory of odors than men, that the primitive olfactory brain, linked to the limbic emotional system, is more highly developed in females. If the emotional and olfactory systems are so linked, it may at least in part explain why women are the more frequent cooks, just as they are the more adept at social facilitation and verbal communication.

CHAPTER TWO

46. "The modern tortilla . . ." Modern pita breads are more often than not lightly leavened with yeast, making them softer and tenderer than their unleavened prototypes. Injera is a spongy, pancakelike bread, traditionally unleavened but made from a fermented bubbly millet batter. Nowadays it is more commonly made from Aunt Jemima pancake mix!

47. "The appropriate ingredients and circumstances . . ." Although in many traditional cultures it was the women who baked the bread and brewed the beer, other societies developed more efficient centralized systems for processing grains. When milling, baking, and brewing were done in the home kitchen, they were done by women; in a more public and central arena they were more often done by men. It is for this reason I have credited Abdoul with the invention of leav-

ened bread, although it is likely to have been an event that occurred many times in the domestic kitchen.

CHAPTER THREE

66. "Indeed, it is entirely possible that the initial exchange . . ." Odd as this practice may seem, it is fairly widespread in rural and traditional cultures. Even in America there is anecdotal evidence from the last hundred or so years for the human suckling of dog pups and other domesticated farm animals. For a complete review see Simoons and Baldwin, "Breast-feeding of Animals by Women: Its Sociocultural Context and Geographic Occurrence."

68. "The answer, as we must have rather quickly discovered . . ." The culturing of milk, with the consequent breakdown of lactose, is another example of the widespread human practice of turning dangerous substances into valuable nourishment by changing or removing toxic elements before the substance is consumed as food. The processing of bitter manioc (cassava) to get rid of prussic acid, the leaching of acorn meal to remove bitter tannins, and the use of heat to destroy dangerous microorganisms are all parallel practices.

74. "It is interesting that while the culturing of milk . . ." E. N. Anderson, in the book *The Food of China*, reports:

"Cheese, however, is usually too much for Chinese to swallow—I have heard it described, to translate roughly, as 'the mucous discharge of some old cow's guts, allowed to putrefy.' "

83. "Indeed, some cuisines have ritualized . . ." The Judaic tradition that makes taboo the mixing of meat and dairy products is based on the biblical stricture "Thou shalt not seethe a kid in its mother's milk," which has been (and continues to be) variously interpreted. It has always seemed to me that the prohibition involves violations in the categories of foodstuffs, one expressed much more directly by the Masai, who believe that the simultaneous consumption of live and dead food (milk and meat) would damage the herds and bring disaster to the people whose lives depend so heavily on their cattle. Similarly, many traditional Eskimo people would not consume food from the land in the same meal as food from the sea, in the belief that to do so would bring grief to the animals and to the people. For an interesting discussion of these issues, see Mary Douglas's book *Purity and Danger*.

CHAPTER FOUR

86. "We don't really know how or why people first began to flavor . . ." It is interesting that the one clear example

of a seasoning practice in animals occurs with the use of salt. A group of monkeys on the Japanese islet of Koshima were fed sweet potatoes by scientists. In the attempt to cleanse the potatoes of sand, the monkeys washed them in fresh water and then switched to seawater. Even when washing the food was no longer necessary, the behavior persisted, particularly by an adult female who taught the practice to younger members of the group. The animals would dip the food in salt water, then take a bite, and it seems clear that the added flavor of salt was crucial to this learned behavior. See M. Kawai, "Newly Acquired Precultural Behavior of the Natural Troop of Japanese Monkeys on Koshima Islet."

92. "The Chinese, for many centuries the widely acknowledged masters . . ." For an interesting discussion of the role of flavor in the Chinese tradition, see Lin and Lin, *Chinese Gastronomy.*

98. "Indeed, some highly orthodox Jewish sects . . ." I learned of the orthodox Jewish reaction to tomatoes from Dr. Barbara Kirschenblatt-Gimblett of New York University, a scholar who specializes in the culture and cuisine of Eastern European Jewry. I subsequently heard of other groups with a similar response, most notably an entire village in Turkey that ate only underripe green tomatoes because the red ripe ones were considered too "bloody."

101. "Indeed, although ketchup's name comes from . . ." It is not entirely clear whether some of the English fish-based fermented sauces, like Worcestershire, entered the tradition at the same time as the ketchups, or were much earlier sauces brought to Britain by the Romans, whose cuisine was based heavily on the fermented fish sauces *garum* and *liquamen*.

104. "Indeed, the English 'sweet tooth' had long been observed and commented on . . ." For a fascinating and thoughtful discussion of sugar and sweetness in the English tradition, so different from the rest of Europe, see Sidney Mintz's *Sweetness and Power*.

CHAPTER FIVE

129. "The pickles on our cheeseburger . . ." As reported in the October 21, 1993, issue of *USA Today*, the dill pickle is the nation's favorite, with a variety of sweet pickles following hard on its heels.

CHAPTER SIX

140. "This practice is extremely widespread . . ." An elegant and extensive description of Bemba food habits is to be

found in Audrey Richards's classic work *Land, Labour and Diet in Northern Rhodesia.*

141. "The dietary principle that describes this balance . . ." For further discussions of the Chinese *fan–ts'ai* system, see E. N. Anderson's *The Food of China* and E. C. Chang's *Food in Chinese Culture.*

CHAPTER SEVEN

168. "What may further account for the strong appeal . . ." For an extensive review of the use and value of sugar in the English tradition, see once again *Sweetness and Power* by Sidney Mintz.

172. "These waters, with their tingly effervescence . . ." Of course, just the opposite may have been true—that is, we may have drunk it first and bathed in it afterward. That seems to have been the case for other parallel situations in which people used foods and drinks to doctor their outsides, as with milk baths, beer shampoos, and cucumber facials.

173. "In this sense, the action of carbonation in liquids is very similar . . ." It is interesting that both chile peppers and carbonation are acquired tastes. The burn of capsaicin and the sting of bubbles are sensations that are generally not

acceptable to babies and young children, who learn to accept and enjoy them through enculturation.

173. "If a pleasant sweet taste and refreshing effervescence were enough . . ." We ingenious humans frequently compound the pharmacologic and medicinal effects of our beverages, as, for example, with the gin and tonic, which combines an antimalarial medication (quinine water) with an intoxicant.

174. "The original formula for Coke . . ." The issue of what makes a drink taste pleasant is complex indeed. While sweet beverages appear to be universally appealing, drinks with a more bitter flavor are also widely attractive. Bitterness seems to be an acquired taste, much more acceptable to adult than to juvenile palates, and this may have to do with the fact that many of our pharmacologic agents are bitter-tasting alkaloids. Coffee, tea, and chocolate are bitter liquids that are often but not always sweetened, while historically beer was deliberately shifted from a mildly sweet to a more bitter profile. It looks as though we must experience our pharmacologically effective beverages as either bitter or sweet. We do not want our beverages to be strongly salty or sour; these tastes are associated with food rather than with drink, and this may be a traditional expression of an ancient awareness that highly concentrated solutions of these substances, such as seawater or acid, can be harmful. When wine becomes sour (in French,

vin aigre), we use the resulting product, vinegar, to flavor food; when we consume a salty liquid, we call it soup and regard it as food. So while a wide range of flavors are acceptable in our food, our beverages are more limited to the bitter and the sweet, with a clearly heavier emphasis on the sweet.

CHAPTER EIGHT

179. "The fried sauced ground beef patty was perceived . . ." For a delightfully nostalgic pictorial review of the hamburger's history in America, see *Hamburger Heaven* by Jeffrey Tennyson.

SELECTED
BIBLIOGRAPHY

Allen, H. Warner. *A History of Wine*. London: Faber and Faber, 1961.

Anderson, E. N. *The Food of China*. New Haven, CT: Yale University Press, 1988.

Anderson, John L., comp. *A Fifteenth Century Cookry Boke*. New York: Scribner's, 1962.

Andrews, Jean. *Peppers: The Domesticated Capsicums*. Austin: University of Texas Press, 1984.

Androuet, P. *Guide du Fromage*. Paris: Stock, 1971.

Apicius. *The Roman Cookery Book*. Translated by Barbara Flower and Elisabeth Rosenbaum. London: Peter Nevill, 1958.

Appadurai, A. "Gastro-politics in Hindu South Asia." *American Ethnologist* 8 (1981): 494–511.

Athenaeus. *The Deipnosophists*. Translated by C. B. Gulick. London and Cambridge, MA: Loeb Classical Library, 1927–41.

Barker, Lewis M., ed. *The Psychobiology of Human Food Selection.* Westport, CT: Avi, 1982.

Beck, S., L. Bertholle, and J. Child. *Mastering the Art of French Cooking.* New York: Knopf, 1963.

Benitez, Ana M. *Pre-Hispanic Cooking.* Mexico City: Euroamericanas, 1974.

Brillat-Savarin, Jean Anthelme. *The Physiology of Taste: Meditations on Transcendental Gastronomy.* New York: Liveright, 1970.

Brothwell, D. R. "Dietary Variation and the Biology of Earlier Human Populations." In *The Domestication and Exploitation of Plants and Animals,* edited by P. J. Ucko and G. W. Dimbleby. Chicago: Aldine, 1969, pp. 531–545.

Brothwell, Don, and Patricia Brothwell. *Food in Antiquity.* New York: Praeger, 1969.

Brown, L. K., and K. Mussell, eds. *Ethnic and Regional Foodways in the United States.* Knoxville: University of Tennessee Press, 1984.

Brown, Robert C. *The Complete Book of Cheeses.* Introduction by Clifton Fadiman. New York: Random House, 1955.

Cain, William S. "Odor Identification by Males and Females: Predictions vs. Performance." *Chemical Senses* 7, no. 2 (1982): 129–142.

Casson, Lionel. *The Ancient Mariners.* New York: Minerva Press, 1959.

Chakravarty, Taponath. *Food and Drink in Ancient Bengal.* Calcutta: P. Chakravarty, 1959.

Chang, E. C., ed. *Food in Chinese Culture.* New Haven, CT: Yale University Press, 1977.

Cheese Varieties and Descriptions. Agriculture Handbook No. 54. Washington, D.C.: U.S. Department of Agriculture, 1969.

Claiborne, Robert. *Climate, Man, and History.* New York: Norton, 1970.

Clair, Colin. *Kitchen & Table.* London: Abelard-Schuman, 1964.

Columbus, Christopher. *The Journal.* Translated by Cecil Jane. New York: Bonanza Books, 1989.

Cooper, James Fenimore. *The Travelling Bachelor, or Notions of the Americans.* New York: Stringer and Townsend, 1856.

Courtine, Robert J. *Larousse des Fromages.* Paris: Librairie Larousse, 1973.

Crosby, Alfred W., Jr. *The Columbian Exchange.* Westport, CT: Greenwood Press, 1972.

Cummings, Richard O. *The American and His Food.* Chicago: University of Chicago Press, 1940.

Cussler, M., and M. L. DeGive. *'Twixt the Cup and the Lip.* New York: Twayne, 1952.

David, Elizabeth. *Spices, Salt and Aromatics in the English Kitchen.* Harmondsworth, Middlesex, England: Penguin Books, 1970.

De Candolle, Alphonse. *Origin of Cultivated Plants*. New York: Hafner, 1959.

de Castro, Josue. *The Geography of Hunger*. Boston: Little, Brown, 1952.

Diaz del Castillo, Bernal. *The Discovery and Conquest of Mexico*. Translated by A. P. Maudslay. New York: Farrar, Straus and Giroux, 1956.

Digby, Joan, and John Digby, eds. *Food for Thought*. New York: William Morrow, 1987.

Douglas, Mary. *Purity and Danger*. New York: Praeger, 1969.

———. "Deciphering a Meal." *Daedalus* 101 (1972): 61–68.

Dumay, Raymond. *Guide des alcools*. Paris: Stock, 1973.

Escoffier, Auguste. *The Escoffier Cook Book*. New York: Crown, 1941.

Farb, P., and G. Armelagos. *Consuming Passions*. Boston: Houghton Mifflin, 1980.

Forbes, M. H. C. "From the Fields of Greece: *Hortopita* (Wild Greens Pie)." In *The Anthropologists' Cookbook*, edited by J. Kuper. New York: Universe Books, 1977, pp. 31–33.

Ford, Barbara. *Future Food*. New York: William Morrow, 1978.

Forde, C. Daryll. *Habitat, Economy and Society*. New York: Dutton, 1963.

Gerard, J. *The Herball*. London, 1633.

Gerbi, Antonello. *Nature in the New World*. Pittsburgh: University of Pittsburgh Press, 1985.

Gernet, Jacques. *Daily Life in China on the Eve of the Mongol Invasion*. New York: Macmillan, 1962.

Graubard, Mark. *Man's Food, Its Rhyme or Reason*. New York: Macmillan, 1943.

Green, Barry G. "The Effects of Temperature and Concentration on the Perceived Intensity and Quality of Carbonation." *Chemical Senses* 17, no. 4 (1992): 435–450.

Grosser, Arthur E. *The Cookbook Decoder*. New York: Beaufort Books, 1981.

Grover, K., ed. *Dining in America 1850–1900*. Amherst, MA: University of Massachusetts Press, 1987.

Guy, Christian. *An Illustrated History of French Cuisine*. New York: Bramhall House, 1962.

Harner, Michael. "The Ecological Basis for Aztec Sacrifice." *American Ethnologist*, vol. 4 (1977): 117–135.

Harris, Marvin. *Cannibals and Kings: The Origins of Cultures*. New York: Random House, 1977.

———. *Cows, Pigs, Wars, and Witches: The Riddles of Culture*. New York: Random House, 1974.

Harris, Marvin, and Eric B. Ross. "How Beef Became King," *Psychology Today*, vol. 12, no. 5 (1978): 88–94.

Harrison, William. *The Description of England*. Edited by Georges Edelen. Ithaca, NY: Folger Shakespeare Library, 1968.

Hartley, Dorothy. *Food in England*. London: Macdonald and Jane's, 1973.

Hayes, Elizabeth S. *Spices and Herbs Around the World*. New York: Doubleday, 1961.

Heiser, Charles B., Jr. *Nightshades: The Paradoxical Plants*. San Francisco: W. H. Freeman, 1969.

Heizer, R. F., and L. K. Napton. "Biological and Cultural Evidence from Prehistoric Human Coprolites." *Science* 165, no. 3893 (1969): 563–568.

Herodotus. *The Histories*. Translated by Aubrey de Selincourt. Baltimore: Penguin Books, 1954.

Hess, John L., and Karen Hess. *The Taste of America*. New York: Grossman, 1977.

Hogg, Garry. *Cannibalism and Human Sacrifice*. London: Robert Hale, 1958.

Jacob H. E. *Six Thousand Years of Bread*. Garden City, NY: Doubleday, Doran, 1944.

Jefferson, Thomas. *Thomas Jefferson's Garden Book*. Annotated by E. M. Bette. Philadelphia: American Philosophical Society, 1944.

Jerome, Carl. *Cooking for a New Earth*. New York: Holt, 1993.

The Jewish Dietary Laws. Revised and expanded edition. New York: Rabbinical Assembly of America and the United Synagogue Commission on Jewish Education, 1982.

Jones, Gwyn. *A History of the Vikings*. London: Oxford University Press, 1973.

Kawai, M. "Newly Acquired Precultural Behavior of the Natural Troop of Japanese Monkeys on Koshima Islet." *Primates* 6 (1965): 1–30.

Kuper, Jessica, ed. *The Anthropologists' Cookbook*. New York: Universe Books, 1977.

Lang, George. *The Cuisine of Hungary*. New York: Bonanza Books, 1971.

la Reynière. *100 Merveilles de la Cuisine Française*. Paris: Seuil, 1971.

Lattimore, Owen, and Eleanor Lattimore, eds. *Silks, Spices and Empire*. New York: Delacorte Press, 1968.

Layton, T. A. *The Cheese Handbook*. New York: Dover, 1973.

Lehner, Ernst, and Johanna Lehner. *Folklore & Odysseys of Food & Medicinal Plants*. New York: Farrar, Straus and Giroux, 1973.

Lévi-Strauss, Claude. *The Raw and the Cooked*. Translated by John and Doreen Weightman. Chicago: University of Chicago Press, 1983.

Lin, Hsiangju, and Tsuifeng Lin. *Chinese Gastronomy*. New York: Hastings House, 1969.

Lin, Tsuifeng, and Hsiangju Lin. *Cooking with the Chinese Flavor*. Englewood Cliffs, NJ: Prentice-Hall, 1956.

Lo, Kenneth. *Chinese Food.* Harmondsworth, Middlesex, England: Penguin Books, 1972.

Lorwin, Madge. *Dining with William Shakespeare.* New York: Atheneum, 1976.

Lu Yu. *The Classic of Tea.* Translated by Francis Ross Carpenter. Boston, Toronto: Little, Brown, 1974.

Mallery, Richard D., ed. *Masterworks of Travel and Exploration.* Garden City, NY: Doubleday, 1948.

McGee, Harold. *On Food and Cooking.* New York: Scribner's, 1984.

Meigs, Anna. *Food, Sex, and Pollution.* New Brunswick, NJ: Rutgers University Press, 1984.

Mintz, Sidney. *Sweetness and Power.* New York: Viking Penguin, 1985.

Montagné, Prosper. *Larousse Gastronomique.* Translated by Froud, Gray, Murdoch, and Taylor. New York: Crown, 1961.

Noss, John B. *Man's Religions.* New York: Macmillan, 1963.

Oakley, Kenneth P. *Man the Tool-Maker.* London: British Museum (Natural History), 1963.

Ottenberg, Simon, and Phoebe Ottenberg, eds. *Cultures and Societies of Africa.* New York: Random House, 1968.

Perl, Lila. *Foods and Festivals of the Danube Lands.* New York: World, 1969.

Phillips, E. D. *The Royal Hordes: Nomad Peoples of the Steppes.* New York: McGraw-Hill, 1965.

Pickersgill, Barbara. "The Domestication of Chile Peppers." In *The Domestication and Exploitation of Plants and Animals*, edited by P. J. Ucko and G. W. Dimbleby. Chicago: Aldine-Atherton, 1969, pp. 443–450.

Piggott, Stuart. *Prehistoric India*. Harmondsworth, Middlesex, England: Penguin Books, 1950.

Pliner, P., and M. L. Pelchat. "Neophobia in Humans and the Special Status of Foods of Animal Origin." *Appetite* 16 (1991): 205–218.

Prakash, Om. *Food and Drinks in Ancient India*. Delhi, India: Munshi Ram Manohar Lal, 1961.

Prentice, E. Parmalee. *Hunger and History*. New York: Harper and Brothers, 1939.

Protsch, R., and R. Berger. "Earliest Radiocarbon Dates for Domesticated Animals." *Science* 179, no. 4070 (1973): 235–239.

Richards, Audrey I. *Hunger and Work in a Savage Tribe*. London: Routledge, 1932.

———. *Land, Labour and Diet in Northern Rhodesia*. London: Oxford University Press, 1939.

Robbins, John. *Diet for a New America*. Walpole, NH: Stillpoint, 1987.

Robbins, Maria P. *The Cook's Quotation Book*. New York: Viking Penguin, 1984.

Root, Waverley, and Richard de Rochemont. *Eating in America: A History*. New York: William Morrow, 1976.

Rorer, Sarah T. *Mrs. Rorer's Cook Book*. Philadelphia: Arnold (no date).

Rosengarten, Frederic, Jr. *The Book of Spices*. New York: Jove, 1981.

Rozin, Elisabeth. "Aesthetics and Cuisine: Mind over Matter." In *Beauty and the Brain*, edited by I. Rentschler, B. Herzberger, and D. Epstein. Basel-Boston-Berlin: Birkhauser Verlag, 1988, pp. 315–325.

———. *Blue Corn and Chocolate*. New York: Knopf, 1992.

———. *Ethnic Cuisine: The Flavor Principle Cookbook*. Brattleboro, VT: Stephen Greene Press, 1983; reprinted as *Ethnic Cuisine*. New York: Viking Penguin, 1992.

———. *The Flavor-Principle Cookbook*. New York: Hawthorn Books, 1973.

———. "The Great Ketchup-Salsa Debate." *Icarus* 9 (1993): 21–27.

———. "Ketchup and the Collective Unconscious." *Journal of Gastronomy* 4, no. 2 (1988): 45–55.

———. "The Structure of Cuisine." In *The Psychobiology of Human Food Selection*, edited by L. M. Barker. Westport, CT: Avi, 1982.

Rozin, E., and P. Rozin. "Culinary Themes and Variations." *Natural History* 90, no. 2 (1981): 6–14.

Rozin, P. "The Selection of Foods by Rats, Humans, and Other Animals." *Advances in the Study of Behavior* 6 (1976): 21–76.

———. "Human Food Selection: The Interaction of Biology, Culture and Individual Experience." In *The Psychobiology of Human Food Selection*, edited by L. M. Barker. Westport, CT: Avi, 1982, pp. 225–254.

Rozin, P., and M. L. Pelchat. "Memories of Mammaries: The Dilemma of Weaning in Mammals." In *Progress in Psychobiology and Physiological Psychology*, edited by A. Epstein and A. Morrison. New York: Academic Press, 1988.

Russell, W. M. S. *Man, Nature and History*. London: Aldus Books, 1967.

Salaman, Redcliffe. *The History and Social Influence of the Potato*. Cambridge, England: Cambridge University Press, 1949.

Sass, Lorna. *To the King's Taste*. New York: Metropolitan Museum of Art, 1975.

———. "Religion, Medicine, Politics and Spices." *Appetite* 2 (1981): 7–13.

Sauer, Carl O. *Land and Life*. Edited by John Leighly. Berkeley and Los Angeles: University of California Press, 1974.

Sauer, Jonathan D. "Changing Perception and Exploitation of New World Plants in Europe, 1492–1800." In *First Images of America*, edited by Fredi Chiappelli. Berkeley and Los Angeles: University of California Press, 1976, pp. 813–832.

Schapira, Joel, David, & Karl. *The Book of Coffee & Tea*. New York: St. Martin's Press, 1975.

Schwabe, Calvin W. *Unmentionable Cuisine*. Charlottesville: University Press of Virginia, 1979.

Shapiro, Laura. *Perfection Salad*. New York: Farrar, Straus and Giroux, 1986.

Sheppard, Ronald, and Edward Newton. *The Story of Bread*. London: Routledge & Kegan Paul, 1957.

Silverberg, Robert. *The Challenge of Climate*. New York: Meredith Press, 1969.

Simoons, Frederick J. *Eat Not This Flesh*. Madison: University of Wisconsin Press, 1961.

———. "Primary Adult Lactose Intolerance and the Milking Habit: A Problem in Biological and Cultural Interrelations II—A Culture Historical Hypothesis." *American Journal of Digestive Diseases* 15 (1970): 695–710.

———. "Geography and Genetics as Factors in the Psychobiology of Human Food Selection." In *The Psychobiology of Human Food Selection*, edited by L. M. Barker. Westport, CT: Avi, 1982, pp. 205–224.

Simoons, F. J., and J. A. Baldwin. "Breast-feeding of Animals by Women: Its Socio-cultural Context and Geographic Occurrence." *Anthropos* 77 (1982): 421–448.

Singh, Dharamijit. *Indian Cookery*. Harmondsworth, Middlesex, England: Penguin Books, 1970.

Smith, Isabel Cotton. *The Blue Book of Cookery*. New York: Funk & Wagnalls, 1926.

Sowell, Thomas. *Ethnic America*. New York: Basic Books, 1981.

Stefansson, Vilhjalmur. *Not by Bread Alone*. New York: Macmillan, 1946.

Struever, Stuart, ed. *Prehistoric Agriculture*. Garden City, NY: Natural History Press, 1971.

Tannahill, Reay. *Food in History*. New York: Stein and Day, 1973.

Tennyson, Jeffrey. *Hamburger Heaven*. New York: Hyperion, 1993.

Treistman, Judith M. *The Prehistory of China*. Garden City, NY: Doubleday, 1972.

Trillin, Calvin. *American Fried*. Garden City, NY: Doubleday, 1974.

Tsuji, Shizuo. *Japanese Cooking: A Simple Art*. Tokyo and New York: Kodansha International, 1980.

Tuorila, H. "Individual and Cultural Factors in the Consumption of Beverages." In *Thirst: Physiological and Psychological Aspects*, edited by D. J. Ramsay and D. Booth. London: Springer-Verlag, 1991, pp. 354–364.

Ucko, P. J., and G. W. Dimbleby, eds. *The Domestication and Exploitation of Plants and Animals*. Chicago: Aldine-Atherton, 1969.

Ukers, William H. *All About Coffee*. New York: Tea & Coffee Trade Journal, 1922.

Vayda, Andrew P., ed. *Environment and Cultural Behavior*. Garden City, NY: Natural History Press, 1969.

Visser, Margaret. *Much Depends on Dinner*. Toronto: McClelland and Stewart, 1986.

———. *The Rituals of Dinner*. New York: Penguin Books, 1992.

Weaver, William W. *Sauerkraut Yankees*. Philadelphia: University of Pennsylvania Press, 1983.

Weiner, Michael A. *Man's Useful Plants*. New York: Macmillan, 1976.

Wheaton, Barbara K. *Savoring the Past*. Philadelphia: University of Pennsylvania Press, 1983.

Woodham-Smith, Cecil. *The Great Hunger*. New York: Harper & Row, 1962.

Woodruff, Jasper G., and G. Frank Phillips, eds. *Beverages: Carbonated and Noncarbonated*. Westport, CT: Avi, 1981.

Yturbide, Teresa Castello. *Presencia de la Comida Prehispanica*. Mexico City: Banamex Fomento Cultural, 1986.

Yudkin, John. "Archaeology and the Nutritionist." In *The Domestication and Exploitation of Plants and Animals*, edited by P. J. Ucko and G. W. Dimbleby. Chicago: Aldine-Atherton, 1969, pp. 547–552.

Zee, A. *Swallowing Clouds*. New York: Simon & Schuster, 1990.

INDEX